# Physical Characteristics of the Irish Terrier

## (from the American Kennel Club breed standard)

**Stern:** Should be docked, taking off about one quarter. It should be set on rather high, but not curled. It should be of good strength and substance; of fair length and well covered with harsh, rough hair.

**Body:** The body should be moderately long. The back must be strong and straight. The loin should be strong and muscular, and slightly arched, the ribs fairly sprung, deep rather than round, reaching to the level of the elbow. The bitch may be slightly longer than the dog.

**Hindquarters:** Should be strong and muscular; thighs powerful; hocks near the ground; stifles moderately bent.

**Coat:** Should be dense and wiry in texture, rich in quality, having a broken appearance, but still lying fairly close to the body, the hairs growing so closely and strongly together that when parted with the fingers the skin is hardly visible; free of softness or silkiness, and not so long as to alter the outline of the body, particularly in the hindquarters.

**Size:** The most desirable weight in show condition is 27 pounds for the dog and 25 pounds for the bitch. The height at the shoulder should be approximately 18 inches.

**Feet and Legs:** The feet should be strong, tolerably round, and moderately small; toes arched and turned neither out nor in, with dark toenails. Legs moderately long, well set from the shoulders, perfectly straight, with plenty of bone and muscle; the elbows working clear of the sides; pasterns short, straight, and hardly noticeable.

c A

# Irish Terrier

◇

## 9

## History of the Irish Terrier

Uncover the mystery of the Irish Terrier's origin, from the breed's generic and humble beginnings to its establishment and acceptance as a pure-bred dog. Did the breed derive from the giant Wolfhound and how colorful was the terrier's past? Find out about early dogs, breeders, service work and what "Billy Graham" has to do with this earthdog!

## 23

## Characteristics of the Irish Terrier

Heads up: enter the Daredevil of the canine world, the Irish Terrier. Meet this boisterous, independent and entertaining terrier whose owners claim that this is a true dog among dogs, unrivaled by other "inferior" terriers. Are you the right owner for this possessive, amazingly loyal and slightly stubborn red dervish?

## 30

## Breed Standard for the Irish Terrier

Learn the requirements of a well-bred Irish Terrier by studying the description of the breed as set forth in the American Kennel Club's breed standard. Both show dogs and pets must possess key characteristics as outlined in the breed standard.

## 36

## Your Puppy Irish Terrier

Be advised about choosing a reputable breeder and selecting a healthy, typical puppy. Understand the responsibilities of ownership, including home preparation, acclimatization, the vet and prevention of common puppy problems.

## 60

## Everyday Care of Your Irish Terrier

Enter into a sensible discussion of dietary and feeding considerations, exercise, grooming, traveling and identification of your dog. This chapter discusses Irish Terrier care for all stages of development.

## 74

## Training Your Irish Terrier

By Charlotte Schwartz
Be informed about the importance of training your Irish Terrier from the basics of house-training and understanding the development of a young dog to executing obedience commands (sit, stay, down, etc.).

# Contents

## Health Care of Your Irish Terrier    **97**

Discover how to select a qualified vet and care for your dog at all stages of life. Topics include vaccinations, skin problems, dealing with external and internal parasites and common medical and behavioral conditions.

## Your Senior Irish Terrier    **128**

Consider the care of your senior Irish Terrier, including the proper diet for a senior. Recognize the signs of an aging dog, both behavioral and medical; implement a special-care program with your vet and become comfortable with making the final decisions and arrangements for your senior Irish Terrier.

## Showing Your Irish Terrier    **134**

Enter the world of showing dogs. Learn about the American Kennel Club, the different types of shows and the making of a champion, and find out about agility and obedience trials and more.

## Behavior of Your Irish Terrier    **142**

Learn to recognize and handle behavioral problems that may arise with your Irish Terrier. Topics discussed include separation anxiety, aggression, barking, chewing, digging, begging, jumping up, etc.

Index . . . . . . . . 156

KENNEL CLUB BOOKS: **IRISH TERRIER**
ISBN: 1-59378-339-6

Copyright © 2003 Kennel Club Books, Inc.
308 Main Street, Allenhurst, NJ 07711 USA
Cover Design Patented: US 6,435,559 B2 • Printed in South Korea

Photos by Carol Ann Johnson with additional photographs by:
Norvia Behling, T.J. Calhoun, Carolina Biological Supply, David Dalton, Doskocil, Isabelle Francais, Freeze Frame, James Hayden-Yoav, James R. Hayden, RBP, Bill Jonas, Dwight R. Kuhn, Dr. Dennis Kunkel, Mikki Pet Products, Phototake, Jean Claude Revy, Dr. Andrew Spielman and Alice van Kempen.
Illustrations by Patricia Peters.

The publisher would like to thank the owners of the dogs featured in this book, including Rejean Charlebois, Pat Dorrian, Mark & Pam Eskridge, Peggy E. Gill, Cheryl Goodfellow, Marianne Kehoe, Jennifer Mulholland-Mousset, Alan Norcross, Paul Richardson and Joyce Wilson.

The Irish Terrier has the reputation of being fiery, boisterous and intelligent, and a faithful family friend. Fanciers around the world prize this native Irish breed. This Canadian record-holder is Am. Can. Ch. Fairplay's Raging Cajun, owned and bred by Cheryle Goodfellow.

# IRISH TERRIER

## THE IRISH MYSTERY

The Irish Terrier has a reputation that precedes him whenever the breed is mentioned. He is the fiery one, boisterous but intelligent, a child's companion, a faithful friend for the elderly. Squirrels and rats are mortal enemies, and cats aren't far behind on the list. With a touch of blarney, he manages to get away with whatever mischief he gets into—and then to make his owner think he's the clever dog for having done it! Beguiling, sparkling, quick to challenge and, with his head on your knee, devotion personified.

The Irish people have always felt strongly about their dogs and, in the Brehon Code dating from the first century A.D., there were rules regarding both the control of dogs and the people's responsibility for them. At that time, all dogs were separated into three categories: hunting dogs, only to be owned by the lords of the land; shepherds' dogs, for guarding the sheep; and small breeds, used primarily as all-around farm dogs. The latter group consisted prima-rily of the terriers, which were dogs owned by the cottagers who worked the land and thus had need of these vermin extermina-tors. (As a sidebar, a quick small terrier, with its strong jaws, was also used for small-game poaching on any nearby land off-limits to the farmer.)

Prior to the 1700s, this mixed bag of terrier-type dogs ran indis-criminately loose, and matings were purely by chance. As time went on, however, dogs became valued solely for their skills and—egotists that people are—were generally referred to by the owner's name. In other words, a dog deemed worthy (or perhaps unworthy) of breeding for its working ability would be spoken of as "O'Brien's Moll" or "Murphy's Dan." It wasn't until dog shows came about in the late 1800s that terriers were lumped together as a group. At first, they were classified more or less by general locale, and dogs called "Irish terriers" came in all manner of sizes and shapes. Specific breed names soon became necessary.

In the beginning, for example, the so-called "Scotch" terrier was any sort of short-legged, long-bodied, rough-coated dog that went to earth after vermin. Over time, these terriers became known as individual breeds—the Scottish Terrier, the West Highland White Terrier and the Cairn Terrier. (The Skye Terrier, despite undergoing several name changes, was always a breed unto itself.) The breed known as the Irish Terrier, as we shall see, began life among that mixed group of terriers native to the Emerald Isle.

Once again, as is the case with the majority of the terrier breeds, we find the history of the breed now known simply as the Irish Terrier to be primarily conjecture. There are those who contend that it stems from the Kerry Blue, and those who would make the same claim in favor of the Irish Soft Coated Wheaten. The fact that these larger terriers, in their colors

*In 1875, there was some dispute over whether "Kate" and "Badger" were of pure Irish blood or were actually red Scottish Terriers.*

of dark blue, brindle, wheaten and red, were to be found throughout Ireland and not in the rest of the British Isles, nor on the Continent (until dog shows came on the scene), would indicate that, whatever their make-up, they could all be considered truly native terriers.

No one goes quite so far as to claim that the Irish Terrier came down solely through the Irish Glen of Imaal Terrier, although an Irish Terrier winner at Lisburn in 1875 was a dog named Stinger, said to have been long-backed, dark-blue grizzle, with short tan legs and white turned-out feet, a description more closely fitting a Glen of Imaal.

Most canine historians agree,

### MEET STONEHENGE

"Stonehenge" was the pseudonym of renowned British dog historian John Henry Walsh (1810–1888). He was a member of Britain's Royal College of Surgeons, but became famous for his interest in, and knowledge of, dogs. His book, *The Dog in Health and Disease*, was such a success that it went to four editions. Another book, *Dogs of the British Islands*, was published in 1867 and was expanded and re-published in five editions. He was also the editor of *The Field*, a country sport publication. He was obviously the right man for his time, and his books have aided historians to this day despite the fact that he was at odds with many regarding the terrier breeds.

however, that what is now called the Irish Terrier (also known as the Red Devil, or Daredevil, if you prefer) was carefully created by man. Originally the breed appeared in every canine color, including white. The first to come into the show ring were black and tan, brindle, wheaten and gray or blue and tan, in addition to the shades of red that we know today as the breed's only acceptable color. The truth may lie in a mix to that dear old dog of yore, which no one can point to with certainty but which almost all terrier people point to with pride: the Old English Black and Tan (which wasn't always black and tan, by the way, nor necessarily English). One writer went so far as to say the Irish Terrier came from a combination of digging terriers from England (and used in the hunt kennels in Ireland), rat dogs found in Cork and "a considerable number of terriers from Wales." Confused? Of course you are. Let's sort out what we can.

Once dogs were separated into specific breeds to facilitate record-keeping for kennel registries and dog shows, with definitive pedigrees required to maintain proof of pure breeding, and with breed standards drawn up to pinpoint what was wanted and what was not, all of this confusion was sorted out. Much of it was conveniently forgotten, but it took time.

## THE COLOR CHART

Irish Terriers were at first accepted in wheaten and gray (or blue) as well as red, but even when breeding only for red or red-wheaten

Irish Terriers of the Red Hill Kennels at work.

The Kerry Blue Terrier, also called the Irish Blue, is larger than the red Irish Terrier.

## THE IRISH WOLFHOUND LEGACY

Many respected Irish terriermen still hold to the Irish Terrier (if not the other three native Irish breeds) as having descended from the Irish Wolfhound, noting that in the beginning it was not uncommon to see Irish Terriers weighing 60 pounds (today's dogs weighing around 25 to 27 pounds.) Looking at these two breeds today, one can see the Wolfhound's lean racy outline reflected in the Irish Terrier, setting it apart from the rest of the long-legged terrier tribe, which tend to be shorter backed, closer coupled and heavier bodied. One might also note that, even today, the Irish Terrier's ears may hang heavily hound-like or folded and thrown back like the Wolfhound's. (Most pups to this day have their ears glued in place

coats, black-and-tan pups often showed up in litters, as they reportedly did in Kerry Blue and Soft Coated Wheaten litters. Those first breeders also noted that the wheaten-colored Irish produced good heads but soft coats, while the deep reds had wiry coats and rather plain heads, said to come from those Old English Black and Tans (or from the Scotch terrier, the Bull-and-Terrier or anything else on which one wanted to pin the blame). No matter. The breeders were determined to breed both red wire coats and good heads.

### HAIL THE KING... AND HIS DOGS!

When King Edward VII returned to London from the country, there were always crowds lining the streets. Following the entourage of ladies-in-waiting and so forth came an omnibus of dogs—Fox Terriers, Irish Terriers, Scottish Terriers and Japanese Spaniels—all standing up on the seats, looking out at the throng of cheering people looking at them! It must have been a comical sight.

to correct these problems.) One may also contend that the large hound's ability to take down a wolf is evident in the tenacity of the red terrier when challenged. But in basic temperament all similarity ends, for the Irish Wolfhound is rightly referred to as the Gentle Giant—a quiet, docile dog—and the Irish Terrier as the reckless Daredevil.

Regardless of how or when they developed separately, the four Irish breeds of terrier—the Irish Terrier, Kerry Blue Terrier (also known as the Irish Blue), Soft Coated Wheaten Terrier and Glen of Imaal Terrier—appear to have been indigenous to Ireland, for no mention is made of them in other lands by the early canine historians such as Stonehenge and Youatt. Not until the third edition of his work, *The Dog in Health and Disease*, published in 1879, did J. H. Walsh ("Stonehenge") include the Irish Terrier, and then only "by request," pointing out his objection to that name for a dog that he felt was simply another variety of the Scotch terrier. (At that time, "Scotch terrier" was a derogatory reference to any terrier that was not a Fox Terrier.) Another writer of the day, Edward C. Ashe, had diverse opinions about many of the breeds and described the Irish Terrier as the "Wild Irishman," whose ancestry was a "mixed bag."

The Soft Coated Wheaten Terrier, another of the terrier breeds native to Ireland.

## ACCEPTANCE AND ESTABLISHMENT OF TYPE IN ITS HOMELAND

The Irish Terrier was accepted for registration by the UK's Kennel Club in 1873, but this was not our lovely present-day Red Devil. The first classes offered were for "Irish Terriers over and under 9 pounds," which gives a fair picture of the motley lot of dogs entered. They were of every color, size and shape. A reporter on the scene summed up the hodge-

The least known of the Irish terrier breeds is the short-legged Glen of Imaal Terrier.

podge by saying that the only thing the dogs had in common was that they were all bred in Ireland!

Adding to the problem of uniformity in the breed's early years was the dispute over what was wanted in the breed. Without a goal, the game was a shambles. What was held in esteem in one region of Ireland was looked upon with disfavor in another. For example, in Ballymena, the preference was for a racy dog, higher on leg and with strong terrier jaws, but carrying a soft wheaten-colored coat. In County Cork, breeders wanted large and light-colored dogs, and, in County Wicklow, breeders opted for a short-legged type. According to early records, one Irish Terrier winner named Slasher was not only white but also was proudly declared by his breeder to have descended from a pure white strain!

Fortunately, there were enough specimens upon which the majority could agree as being examples of what was wanted in the breed, and they set the type that prevailed. One such good example was George Jamison's Sport, a dog said to be of the right size and color, with naturally correct ears. He must have appeared too extreme for the judges of the day, as he did not do much winning. The breeders, however, liked what they saw and what the dog produced.

Gradually, what pleased the discerning eye prevailed and the Irish Terrier separated itself once and for all from the Kerry Blue (or Irish Blue), from the Soft Coated Wheaten and from the short-legged Glen of Imaal, to take its place as a separate, worthy, competitive Irish show dog while retaining all of its terrier fire.

George Krehl and fellow Irish Terrier exhibitor and author, James Watson, were said to be instrumental in putting together the breed standard. Every breed new to the dog show scene has had its publicist, and Mr. Krehl was one who promoted the Irish Terrier in its infancy. In 1894, the noted terrier expert, Rawdon B. Lee, did even more to further the popularity of the Irish Terrier in numerous articles and in a volume of *Modern Dogs* devoted

---

### WHERE'S THE RED?

As early as 1847, a Dubliner, H. D. Richardson, described a Harlequin Terrier as "bluish-slate, marked with darker blotches and patches and often with tan about the muzzle." He pointed out its great skill at pursuing and dispatching game, but apparently this particular dog went the way of all things. Strangely, however, in his writings about all the terriers of Ireland, Richardson does not even once mention a red Irish Terrier!

## SLIGHTLY CROSSED?

Many of the terrier breeds were at first openly referred to as cross-breeds. As late as 1859, Stonehenge wrote of the Fox Terrier as being "slightly crossed with the bull-dog in order to give courage to bear the bites of the vermin which they are meant to attack." Today, use of the term "slightly crossed" in the pure-bred world would set off bells and whistles!

to terriers. Almost 100 years later, the noted terrierman, judge and author, Tom Horner, went even further to suggest that Rawdon Lee may actually have been the author of the Irish Terrier breed standard, since it was said to have been drawn up by an "up-to-date but anonymous admirer and successful breeder of the variety." This description not only describes Mr. Lee but the standard also was first mentioned in Mr. Lee's book.

In 1894, the Irish Terrier Club was formed in a rather unique fashion, with two secretaries—Dr. R. B. Carey in Ireland and Mr. A. W. Krehl in England—and two vice-presidents—again one Irish and one English—plus a committee of 20. Mr. C. J. Barnett, an Irish Terrier breeder, ardently backed by George Krehl, began a movement to ban ear cropping and in

Ch. Sporter, owned by the great breed enthusiast George W. Krehl, was exhibited in Ireland and won many first prizes in shows throughout the country.

Artist R. H. Moore's rendering of E. A. Wiener's Ch. Brickbat, one of the last successful crop-eared dogs in the breed.

1880 offered at least one prize to the best Irish Terrier with uncropped ears. Seven years later, no prizes or cups (other than the Club's Challenge Cup for Best of Breed) were to be awarded any Irish Terrier whelped after July of that year if the ears were cropped. In 1889, The Kennel Club ruled that no Irish Terrier whelped after December 31, 1899 could compete in its licensed shows if cropped. This was the first such ruling, which eventually led to a ban on cropping in all breeds.

One famous dog just made the cut (no pun intended). Ch. Brickbat did have cropped ears, but got by on his birthdate and went on to win the Breeder's Cup 12 times in a row, starting in 1889.

### THE BREED'S TRUE FOUNDATION

The Man of the Hour was William Graham, known as "Billy Graham, the Irish Ambassador,'" a reference to his breeding of numerous top dogs and to his wide travels in pursuit of establishing the breed. This Belfast breeder is acknowledged to be the one person who perfected the look of the Irish Terrier we see today.

In 1879, two Irish Terriers, Billy Graham's Ch. Erin and Mr. Waterhouse's Ch. Killiney Boy, not only became prominent in their day but also ever since have been considered the true "parents" of the breed. Their offspring included numerous champions. It was well known that Killiney Boy's dam was a black-and-tan bitch, though he was a solid red. This color purification process occurred in numerous breeds that were being refined, or made uniform, for the show ring.

Both Erin and Killiney Boy had cropped ears. Erin was high on leg, with a good head and soft coat. Killiney Boy had the right coat and head, but was shorter on leg. A perfect match! Ch. Erin

### STONEHENGE'S RECOGNITION

It wasn't until 1879 that the renowned canine historian added the Irish Terrier to his list of terriers, and indicated red, yellow or gray as acceptable colors. At this time, he stated that the breed was descended from the Scotch terrier, adding that it was said to have been pure-bred in Ireland since about 1830.

bred to Ch. Killiney Boy produced a remarkable litter of show winners—Playboy, Pretty Lass, Poppy, Pagan II, Peggy and Gerald. Some of them carried the grandmother's black-and-tan coloration, but two pure reds—Poppy and Playboy—went far in establishing breed type. Over 90% of all Irish Terriers can be traced back to this litter.

In the next few years, colors other than red or wheaten were emphatically excluded from breeding programs and few appeared thereafter in the show ring.

## WAR SERVICE
The Irish Terrier served as messenger and sentinel in World War I, putting the breed's fearless spirit and noted loyalty to good use. Lt. Col. E. H. Richardson, who became Commandant of the British War-Dog School, noted in an article about the breed, "I can say with decided emphasis that the Irish Terriers of the service

more than did their part. My opinion of this breed is indeed a high one." Adding, "They are highly sensitive, spirited dogs of fine mettle, and those of us who respect and admire the finer qualities of mind will find them amply reflected in these Terriers. They are extraordinarily intelligent, faithful, and honest, and a man who has one of them as a companion will never lack a true friend."

By the end of World War I, Irish Terrier breeders were claiming larger stud fees and getting top prices for their pups. Many—especially dogs that were already champions—were sold abroad, becoming the breed's foundation in Europe, America and Canada. Obviously, this sudden popularity was due in great part to the breed's striking good looks. The era of pet ownership was erupting and little thought therefore was given to utilizing the Irish Terrier's natural skills and instincts.

Ch. Playboy, from the remarkable and successful litter by Mr. William "Billy" Graham's Killiney Boy out of Erin.

## THE IRISH ARRIVES IN AMERICA

By 1881, the Irish Terrier was already on its way in the United States with classes at the Westminster Kennel Club show in New York City, although it was another 15 years before the Irish Terrier Club of America was founded and the British standard officially adopted by the American Kennel Club (to be revised in 1929 and in 1968). The Red Devil quickly gained popularity, however, and by 1929 was ranked 13th of the breeds then recognized by the American Kennel Club.

Jeremiah ("Jerry") O'Callaghan, was born in County Cork in 1886, emigrated to America at the age of 11 and became the single most important breeder of Irish Terriers in the US at the turn of the century. The foundation of his Kilvara line was from Celtic Badger, a dog his uncle, a priest in Canada,

purchased on a visit to Ireland. Jerry died in 1973, having outlived the first lot of American breeders who were his competition, but having started many important new kennels such as Aroostock and Ahtram with his Kilvara stock.

The Irish Terrier in the United States has been small in number of late, but in good shape and with many long-time fanciers. Two such people were Michael and Mary Gately, who came to New York from Ireland and began their Blazer kennels in the 1940s with Ch. Galway Blazer, a winner over a breed entry of 63 at Westminster in 1944. A highlight of Michael Gately's lifetime involvement in the breed came in 1972, when he was invited to judge Irish Terriers at the Dublin St. Patrick's Day show.

At the Montgomery County show, the most prestigious all-terrier show in North America (with huge numbers of overseas visitors each year who would agree), the Irish Terrier has had

Ch. Breda Mixer, bred by Billy Graham in 1889, was a prolific winner and one of the most important Irish Terriers of that time.

better success in Group placement than in capturing Best In Show. In 1940, Ch. Newtownards Aristocrat was the first Irish to go to the top, handled by one of America's leading terriermen, George Ward. In 1950, Stately Lady, a young bitch not yet a champion, took Best in Show, handled by the renowned Irish Terrier breeder and handler Ed (Pop) Sayres, Sr. After that, there was a very long dry spell until Ch. Rough and Ready's Wild Irishman went the distance in 1994, followed by the win in 1998 of Ch. Rockledge's Mick of Meath, bred and owned by Linda Honey and the late Marion Honey. Marion was another lifelong breeder and proponent of the breed. Her Rockledge kennels have world-wide recognition.

Two additional leading American kennels, which have consistently produced excellent specimens for many decades, are Jeanene MacDonald's Mullaghboy in California and Cocksure, owned by the terrier handler and judge Robert Clyde.

## SUCCESSES IN IRELAND AND BEYOND

Two pairs of father-son Irish Terrier breeders came together when Ch. Edbrios Dirmuid took the Terrier Group at the Irish Kennel Club Top Irish Showdog of the Year Final in 1998. Dirmuid was bred by father Ed O'Brien and his son Philip, who handled for

Ch. Fairywell's Sergeant Pepper, a favorite dog of Irish breeder Pat Dorrian, now in Germany.

the win. Paul Sweeney made the first presentation of a perpetual trophy for the Top Terrier in memory of his father, Gerry Sweeney, a lifetime Irish breeder. It was fitting that this initial trophy should go first to Dirmuid, an Irish Terrier. Sweeney's Ch. Teltown General McKee was Ireland's Dog of the Year in 1976, also taking Best of Breed at Crufts that year. Afterward, he went to Countess Stuaffenberg in Germany. Paul Sweeney is carrying on the family's Teltown Irish Terrier breeding.

According to Phil O'Brien, Ir. Eng. and Int. Ch. Edbrios Dirmuid not only excels in conformation

### AWAY FROM HOME
The first Irish Terrier to appear in a show ring outside Ireland was in a dog show in Glasgow, Scotland in 1875. Unfortunately, full information about this momentous entry is lost.

Pat Dorrian of County Antrim, Northern Ireland, showing at Crufts, the UK's largest dog show.

but also is as much fun to live with as he is to show. Another top dog from this kennel was Eng. Ch. Edbrios Duplicate, with an enviable record of Top Sire in the UK from 1991 through 1998. This dog made quite an impact on the breed and was used extensively in the UK and on the Continent. Four of the five champions made up in the UK in 1999 had Duplicate behind them.

Pat Dorrian (Fairywells) of County Antrim in Northern Ireland claims Mr. T. Watterson (Esperon) as his mentor since the first Irish pup he purchased as a pet became Eng. Ch. Esperon's Hillside Sandy. Not a bad start! There followed many more good dogs, with two favorites—Ch. Fairywell's Sergeant Pepper and his daughter Ch. Kentee Begraceful of Fairywells. Dorrian shows and judges in the UK and continental Europe.

The Irish Terrier has been well accepted outside its homeland, without becoming overly popular anywhere, for which the breeders are eternally thankful. Excessive public admiration and demand generally lead to overbreeding, with many puppies going to inappropriate, uninformed homes which, in turn, leads to a glut of dogs in need of new homes, to the detriment of the breed and its reputation.

A leading Canadian breeder in British Columbia is Cheryle Goodfellow. Dogs from her Fairplay kennels led the breed in 1993, 1994, 1995, 1997 and 1998. Many have earned championships on both sides of the border, notably Am. Can. Ch. Fairplay's Raging Cajun, the Number One Terrier in Canada in 1995. Another dual champion and big winner in Canada is Ch. Windeire Northern Jet Stream, owned by Ian and Pat MacDonald of Ontario.

The breed's successes outside Ireland do not stop in North America, as the breed has found devotees on the Continent as well. Finland is well represented in the breed by Am. Fin. Est. Ch. Kelson's Tralee Benchmark (a.k.a. Morgan), a dog bred by Amy and Minor Sumners in the United States. Morgan was Finland's Number One Irish Terrier in 1999 while living with Jetta Tschokkinen of the Fardarrigh kennels.

In Sweden, the Merrymac kennels are justly proud of Nor. Dual Ch. Merrymac Magical Michael, a Group 3 winner in the Vaxjo International Show under an Irish judge.

One would have to say that, world-wide, the Irish Terrier is in good shape. He is not overly popular but is well loved as a pet, with few if any variances as a show dog and with no breed-specific inherited health problems.

Irish Terriers are known for being active, feisty, working dogs, but they are equally devoted as family companions and enjoy the comforts of home.

# IRISH TERRIER

The Irish Terrier did not originate as a small dog meant to sit by the fire, warming his feet! These larger terriers were a hardened lot, following the farmer during the day and playing with the children whenever the opportunity presented itself, but always, always on the lookout for the unwary rat or the approaching stranger. At night, they became solitary watchmen, left alone outdoors with no one to tell them what to do or when to do it, but alert to every stealthy movement of nocturnal vermin nearing the potato pit.

This living arrangement, for the most part, led to the dogs' choosing their own mates. Only a farmer's bragging about his dog's skills improved the dog's chances of being purposely mated to a like individual in the vicinity. This is how the intelligence and keen working ability of the breed was set.

With the advent of dog shows, and a monetary value being placed on a "well-bred" dog, came an end to such casual breeding practices. Controlled mating was essential to establish and maintain the individual breeds. A crucial outcome of this for the Irish Terrier, in addition to uniformity of appearance, was setting a standard for desirable temperament. These dogs were now in demand as family pets, not nocturnal Nimrods.

## PERSONALITY
The AKC breed standard describes the Irish Terrier as being "of good temper, most affectionate and absolutely loyal to mankind." Interesting to note is that the British standard expands a bit on this, including that the breed is "perhaps a little too ready to resent interference on the part of other dogs." The AKC standard also states, "There is a heedless, reckless pluck about the Irish Terrier, which is characteristic, and, coupled with the headlong dash, blind to all consequences, with which he rushes at his adversary, has earned for the breed the proud epithet of 'Daredevil.'" The one word "hoydenish"—with its connotation of boisterous, bold or tomboyish behavior—might best describe this side of the

breed's personality.

That description alone should make it clear why this is not a breed for the timid, the weak-willed or those who merely wish to pamper a pet and be pampered in return. The breed's reckless pluck has been toned down a great deal for its present primary role as a pet, while the breed retains to a lesser extent the instinctive drives of its ancestors. However, the Irish Terrier should not be thought of as anything more than assertive. He is not aggressive toward people, but he is a dog who likes who he is and doesn't mind letting others know it. (Cats and other dogs, particularly same-sex dogs, should keep their distance!) The Irish may even appear a bit cautious or reserved when meeting strangers, which makes a very nice first impression. However, the unwary intruder will be met with growls, lunging and an exposed set of very large, strong teeth. The Irish is perhaps the premier guardsman of the terrier tribe.

The other side of the Irish Terrier's canine coin are his virtues as an affectionate, loyal, tender, devoted companion and guardian. He has been described as "the poor man's sentinel, the farmer's friend and the gentleman's favorite." One might only add the children's best playmate.

Clearly the red terrier is a

**TWO IRISH RULES**

There are two rules for obedience training an Irish Terrier. First, be patient. And second, smile! Be patient until the dog figures out what it is you want of him, and smile because it shows the dog he has pleased you (he may smile back!). Harsh corrections will be met with resistance. Disregard these rules and you'll be in for a frustrating time of it.

dog of diverse characteristics. He is first and foremost a speedy, still somewhat reckless, fearless, fired-up terrier. That is his innate mental base of operation, which coordinates well with his role as an excellent guard dog. The Irish Terrier will take a firm stand over his home and family against all that may threaten either one. Fortunately for the pet owner, he also has a good-natured, even-tempered side to him, which is the breeder's duty to uphold and the owner's responsibility to bring out, nurture and maintain.

An utterly charming facet of the breed is its smile. If you have not seen it before, you may think that the dog is baring his teeth in hostility, but nothing could be further from the truth—Irish Terriers can and do smile! After a day's work, nothing is more pleasant than to be welcomed by an "Irish smile."

For the sportsman, a properly trained Irish Terrier is also considered an excellent dog in the field, said to be curious, bright, hardy and sensible, easily trained to perform many spaniel skills such as flushing birds. He is steady under the gun, and retrieves from both land and water. It's a pity that not many Irish Terriers today are given the opportunity to prove these capabilities.

There was a period after World War I during which breeding for correct temperament was abandoned in favor of perfecting the visible qualities wanted in the show ring. The breed went downhill in short order, with many specimens exhibiting shyness, instability and even timidity—all traits totally foreign to the Irish Terrier. It was character assassination! Once those alien quirks were eliminated, the breed got back on track and the typical outgoing Irish "cock-of-the-walk" attitude returned.

Today's Irish Terrier is a wonderful mix of boundless energy with a fearless "I can do it" attitude, combined with a charming and disarming gentleness. He is a loving, loyal, personable dog. He is a good judge of character which, combined with the fact that he is not rowdy, enables him to excel as a guard dog. When the Irish barks, his owner does well to listen. He still is game and ready to tackle trouble, but he is also ready for anything his owner has in mind, be it a serious walk down the city street to show off his marvelous good looks and accept admiring glances, or to play with the children in the park or to go for a walk in the

Those large terrier teeth need to keep busy! Plenty of activity and proper chew toys are recommended to give your Irish outlets for his energy and prevent him from sinking his chops into something he finds in the yard.

country. (In order of preference, the dog might well put that last offer first.)

## TRAINABILITY

It goes without saying that the Irish Terrier is easily aroused to chase a squirrel (or the neighbor's cat), but he is also an intelligent dog and this combination requires consistent good-natured training, lest he should decide to take charge and run the show his way. Intelligence in any terrier is a challenge to the pet owner as well as to many dog trainers, because it conflicts with the way most other breeds are taught and the way in which they learn.

Once your Irish Terrier has correctly performed the lesson you are teaching him, he will not repeat it over and over again just for the joy of pleasing you. His logical mind tells him that there is more to life than six perfect sits. So he becomes what we in terriers prefer to call "inventive" (trainers have other words for it!). He is not being stubborn, stupid or naughty, but merely doing the same thing differently or doing something else entirely. He is only trying to prove to you how clever he can be. Trainers tend not to be awe-struck by such canine cleverness...but laugh and your Irish will laugh with you!

The average Irish can come up with numerous variations to liven up a boring lesson. The trick, therefore, is to prevent boredom from setting in. One or two perfect responses in a brief training session will let you know he has made the connection, and your approval will let the dog know he has done as you asked. Working for 10 or 15 minutes 2 or 3 times a day is a better schedule for an Irish than half an hour or more once a day.

One must never, ever, be physically harsh in training these dogs. Simply put: Don't mess with those teeth! A sharp tone of voice is evidence enough of your disapproval. "Gentle but firm" is the terrier training motto—gentle in physical corrections, and firm in your determination to be the master.

Then there are the all-day, everyday lessons. For example, an excellent way to teach a puppy to come when called is to say "Where are you?" (with a big smile and outstretched arms) each and every time he happens to be walking or running toward you. (This works better than the word "come" with most dogs.) Of course, the real trick when applied to an Irish Terrier is to keep repeating it until he is two or three years old! It's that independent intelligence that makes all terriers decide when they will and when they won't obey. It's a result of having originally been bred to work on their own,

When Irish eyes are smiling! One look from this charmer and you just might forget any mischief he may have gotten himself into.

**BATTLE OF THE TERRIERS?**
The Irish Terrier was used during both World Wars by both sides. The English and the Germans both thought highly of the breed's exceptional skills as messengers and sentinels. Fortunately, dogs are apolitical, but it's tempting to envision how two Irish Terriers from opposing forces would have reacted had they met on the battle-field. A third world war perhaps?

but personally I think now they just do it to keep us on our toes. It's the twinkle in their eyes that betrays them (plus an occasional "smile").

### HOME IS HIS CASTLE

The Irish Terrier can call almost anywhere home. From an apartment in the city to suburban sprawl to—well, back to the farm—the Irish will settle in easily to guard his home and family. A city dog will require more walks, preferably as many as possible in the park. The suburban dog is prime for sufficient training to be a good neighbor. A country dog may need restraining lest he revert to his indigenous ways of staying out all night. But then, life in the country will let him get back to nature—that is, to hunt small game (rabbits are a favorite sport), and there is always the odd mouse or rat to dispatch. He is an accomplished sportsman and he is not gun-shy.

The Irish Terrier is tolerant of other pets in the home, but can be easily fired up if another animal shows any sign of dominance. Some Irish (albeit not many!) have been known to live compatibly with cats if raised with them. Small creatures such as pet mice or guinea pigs do not stand a chance under the same roof as an Irish. There's a joke among Irish Terrier fanciers: "They're friendly with other animals—that is, if the other animal is submissive or dead." Not entirely true, but a clear indication of the breed's assertive nature. It doesn't take much on the part of another animal to get the Irish's dander up. He has a very high opinion of himself and expects others to take note. Breeders generally find they can run several dogs together.

### TYPICAL IRISH ANTICS

The Irish is quite capable of making himself at home just about anywhere you wish to take him. Occasionally, it's too much of a good thing. A prolonged visit with Aunt Mary may find "Paddy" curled up asleep on her bed!

For about a month, "Boggs," an Irish Terrier, shared my home with "Sara," a Welsh Terrier. Boggs would wait until Sara had settled into a comfy chair and then, with an outburst of barking, dash across the room, at which point the Welsh would join in pursuit of what must be wolves at the door and Boggs would race back to claim the prized spot on the chair. Such was the authenticity of his "alarm bark" that the game lasted his entire stay.

## THE CHILDREN'S PLAYMATE

Dedication to the breed is unswerving. It has proven itself to be one of the breeds you grow up with as a child, acquire for your own children and continue on with an Irish by your side for the rest of your life. And Irish Terrier loyalty goes both ways.

The Irish is a fun-loving dog and makes a wonderful playmate for children. When play becomes too rough or boisterous, however, the dog (and/or the kids) will need a time-out to restore peace, or perhaps to prevent a war. Squealing voices, small legs on the run and arms waving in the air may all be too enticing for a terrier's mouth. Older children of eight or nine years of age are considered by most good breeders to be the right age to do their share in the care and training of an Irish puppy.

### DOGS, DOGS, GOOD FOR YOUR HEART!

People usually purchase dogs for companionship, but studies show that dogs can help to improve their owners' health and level of activity, as well as lower a human's risk of coronary heart disease. Without even realizing it, when a person puts time into exercising, grooming and feeding a dog, he also puts more time into his own personal health care. Dog owners establish more routine schedules for their dogs to follow, which can have positive effects on their own health. Dogs also teach us patience, offer unconditional love and provide the joy of having a furry friend to pet!

# IRISH TERRIER

## INTRODUCTION TO THE BREED STANDARD

A breed standard is merely a word description that covers every facet of what is wanted in the breed in question, both physically and temperamentally. The Irish Terrier breed standard particularly spells out in great detail the desired temperament of the breed. In the case of the Irish Terrier, there is good reason to go beyond the conformation, or physical picture, of the perfect dog.

The breed is the personification of "terrier," or what people think of as "terrier temperament" raised to the maximum. Throwing caution to the wind is just one side of the breed's character. The other side is the dog's mellow attitude with humans. The British standard, which is that used in the breed's homeland, Ireland, explains it especially well: "Characterised by a quiet, caress-inviting appearance" and "endearingly, timidly pushing their heads into their masters' hands." This detailed description of the breed's dual personality is essential, because it is in large part what makes an Irish an Irish! A fearful, bashful Irish Terrier is an oxymoron.

In conformation, the trim racy outline of the Irish distinguishes him from other terriers. A short, cobby dog is highly undesirable. The head is also long, in balance with the racy outline. At approximately 18 inches tall at the shoulder, a dog should weigh about 27 pounds and a bitch 25 pounds.

A breed standard details what every breeder should aim for and what every conformation judge should look for—the perfect breed specimen. But we must settle for coming close, since we know that true perfection does not exist in nature.

## THE AMERICAN KENNEL CLUB BREED STANDARD FOR THE IRISH TERRIER

**Head:** Long, but in nice proportion to the rest of the body; the skull flat, rather narrow between the ears, and narrowing slightly toward the eyes; free from wrinkle, with the stop hardly noticeable except in profile. The jaws must be strong and muscular, but not too full in the cheek, and of good punishing length. The foreface must not fall away appreciably between or below the eyes; instead, the modeling should be delicate. An exaggerated foreface, or a noticeably short foreface, disturbs the proper balance of the head and is not desirable. The foreface and the skull from occiput to stop should be approximately equal in length. Excessive muscular development of the cheeks, or bony development of the temples, conditions which are described by the fancier as "cheeky," or "strong in head," or "thick in skull" are objectionable. The "bumpy" head, in which the skull presents two lumps of bony structure above the eyes, is to be faulted. The hair on the upper and lower jaws should be similar in quality and texture to that on the body, and of sufficient length to present an appearance of additional strength and finish to the foreface. Either the profuse, goat-like beard, or the absence of beard, is unsightly and undesirable.

**Teeth:** Should be strong and even, white and sound; and neither overshot nor undershot.

**Lips:** Should be close and well-fitting, almost black in color.

**Profile of an Irish Terrier of correct type, balance and structure.**

**Nose:** Must be black.

**Eyes:** Dark brown in color; small, not prominent; full of life, fire and intelligence, showing an intense expression. The light or yellow eye is most objectionable, and is a bad fault.

**Ears:** Small and V-shaped; of moderate thickness; set well on the head, and dropping forward closely toward the outside corner of the eye. The top of the folded ear should be well above the level of the skull. A "dead" ear, hound-like in appearance, must be severely penalized. It is not characteristic of the Irish Terrier. The hair should be much shorter and somewhat darker in color than that on the body.

**Neck:** Should be of fair length and gradually widening toward the shoulders; well and proudly carried, and free from throatiness. Generally there is a slight frill in the hair at each side of the neck, extending almost to the corner of the ear.

**Study of correct head in profile.**

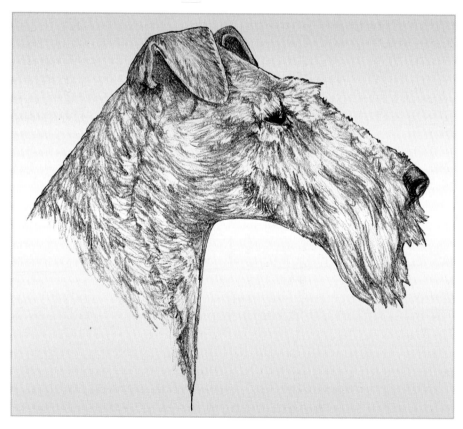

**Shoulders and Chest:** Shoulders must be fine, long, and sloping well into the back. The chest should be deep and muscular, but neither full nor wide.

**Body:** The body should be moderately long. The short back is not characteristic of the Irish Terrier, and is extremely objectionable. The back must be strong and straight, and free from an appearance of slackness or "dip" behind the shoulders. The loin should be strong and muscular, and slightly arched, the ribs fairly sprung, deep rather than round, reaching to the level of the elbow. The bitch may be slightly longer than the dog.

**Hindquarters:** Should be strong and muscular; thighs powerful; hocks near the ground; stifles moderately bent.

**Stern:** Should be docked, taking off about one quarter. It should be set on rather high, but not curled. It should be of good strength and substance; of fair length and well covered with harsh, rough hair.

**Feet and Legs:** The feet should be strong, tolerably round, and moderately small; toes arched and turned neither out nor in, with dark toenails. The pads should be deep, and must be perfectly sound and free from corns. Cracks alone do not necessarily indicate unsound feet. In fact, all breeds have cracked pads

Correct ear size, placement and carriage.

Ears too small and high set; more appropriate for a Wire Fox Terrier.

Ears too large, set apart and carried too low; bumpy skull.

Incorrect fly-away ear carriage.

occasionally, from various causes.

Legs moderately long, well set from the shoulders, perfectly straight, with plenty of bone and muscle; the elbows working clear of the sides; pasterns short, straight, and hardly noticeable. Both fore and hind legs should move straight forward when traveling; the stifles should not turn outward. "Cowhocks"—that is, the hocks turned in and the feet turned out— are intolerable. The legs should be free from feather and covered with

## FAULTS IN PROFILE

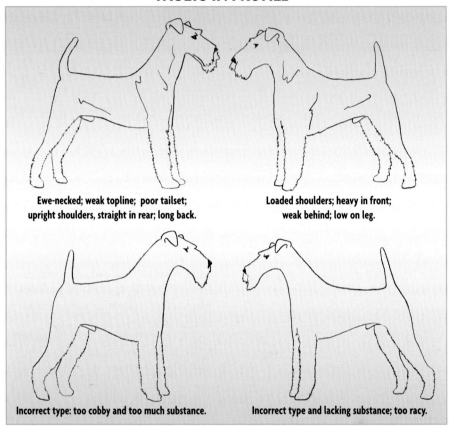

Ewe-necked; weak topline; poor tailset; upright shoulders, straight in rear; long back.

Loaded shoulders; heavy in front; weak behind; low on leg.

Incorrect type: too cobby and too much substance.

Incorrect type and lacking substance; too racy.

hair of similar texture to that on the body to give proper finish to the dog.

**Coat:** Should be dense and wiry in texture, rich in quality, having a broken appearance, but still lying fairly close to the body, the hairs growing so closely and strongly together that when parted with the fingers the skin is hardly visible; free of softness or silkiness, and not so long as to alter the outline of the body, particularly in the hindquarters. On the sides of the body the coat is never as harsh as on the back and quarters, but it should be plentiful and of good texture. At the base of the stiff outer coat there should be a growth of finer and softer hair, lighter in color, termed the undercoat. Single coats, which are without any undercoat, and wavy coats are undesirable; the curly and the kinky coats are most objectionable.

**Color:** Should be whole-colored: bright red, golden red, red wheaten, or wheaten. A small patch of white on the chest, frequently encountered in all whole-colored breeds, is permissible but not desirable. White on any other part of the body is most objectionable. Puppies sometimes have black hair at birth, which should disappear before they are full grown.

**Size:** The most desirable weight in show condition is 27 pounds for the dog and 25 pounds for the bitch. The height at the shoulder should be approximately 18 inches. These figures serve as a guide to both breeder and judge. In the show ring, however, the informed judge readily identifies the oversized or undersized Irish Terrier by its conformation and general appearance. Weight is not the last word in judgment. It is of the greatest importance to select, insofar as possible, terriers of moderate and generally accepted size, possessing the other various characteristics.

**General Appearance:** The overall appearance of the Irish Terrier is important. In conformation he must be more than a sum of his parts. He must be all-of-a piece, a balanced vital picture of symmetry, proportion and harmony. Furthermore, he must convey character. This terrier must be active, lithe and wiry in movement, with great animation; sturdy and strong in substance and bone structure, but at the same time free from clumsiness, for speed, power and endurance are most essential. The Irish Terrier must be neither "cobby" nor "cloddy," but should be built on lines of speed with a graceful, racing outline.

**Temperament:** The temperament of the Irish Terrier reflects his early background: he was a family pet, guard dog, and hunter. He is good tempered, spirited and game. It is of the utmost importance that the Irish Terrier show fire and anima-tion. There is a heedless, reckless pluck about the Irish Terrier which is characteristic, and which, coupled with the headlong dash, blind to all consequences, with which he rushes at his adversary, has earned for the breed the proud epithet of "Daredevil." He is of good temper, most affectionate, and absolutely loyal to mankind. Tender and forebearing with those he loves, this rugged, stout-hearted terrier will guard his master, his mistress and children with utter contempt for danger or hurt. His life is one continuous and eager offering of loyal and faithful companionship and devotion. He is ever on guard, and stands between his home and all that threatens.

*Approved December 10, 1968.*

# IRISH TERRIER

## SELECTING A BREEDER AND PUPPY

If you are convinced that the Irish Terrier is the ideal dog for you, it's time to learn about where to find a puppy and what to look for. You should inquire about breeders who enjoy a good reputation in the breed. You are looking for an established breeder with outstanding dog ethics and a strong commitment to the breed. New owners should have as many

Irish Terrier pups at four to five weeks of age, sired by Ch. Montelle Famous Star out of Ch. Kentee Begraceful.

> **TEMPERAMENT COUNTS**
> Your selection of a good puppy can be determined by your needs. A show potential or a good pet? It is your choice. Every puppy, however, should be of good temperament. Although show-quality puppies are bred and raised with emphasis on physical conformation, responsible breeders strive for equally good temperament. Do not buy from a breeder who concentrates solely on physical beauty at the expense of personality.

questions as they have doubts. An established breeder is indeed the one to answer your four million questions and make you comfortable with your choice of the Irish Terrier. An established breeder will sell you a puppy at a fair price if, and only if, the breeder determines that you are a suitable, worthy owner of his dogs. An established breeder can be relied upon for advice, no matter what time of day or night. A reputable breeder will accept a puppy back, without questions, should you decide that this is not the right dog for you.

When choosing a breeder, reputation is much more important than convenience of location. Do not be overly impressed by breeders who run brag advertisements in the dog presses about their stupendous champions. The real quality breeders are quiet and unassuming. You hear about them at the dog shows and obedience trials, by word of mouth. You may be well advised to avoid the novice breeder, who, trying so hard to get rid of that first litter of puppies, is more than accommodating and anxious to sell you one. That breeder will charge you as much as any established breeder. The novice breeder isn't going to interrogate you and your family about your intentions with the puppy, the environment and training you can provide, etc. That breeder will be nowhere to be found when your poorly bred, badly adjusted four-pawed monster starts to growl and spit up at midnight or eat the family cat!

Choosing a breeder is an important first step in dog ownership. Fortunately, the majority of Irish Terrier breeders is very devoted to the breed and its well-being. New owners should have little problem finding a reputable breeder who doesn't live on the other side of the country. The American Kennel Club is able to refer you to breeders of quality Irish Terriers, as can an Irish

### ARE YOU PREPARED?

Unfortunately, when a puppy is bought by someone who does not take into consideration the time and attention that dog ownership requires, it is the puppy who suffers when he is either abandoned or placed in a shelter by a frustrated owner. So all of the "homework" you do in preparation for your pup's arrival will benefit you both. The more informed you are, the more you will know what to expect and the better equipped you will be to handle the ups and downs of raising a puppy. Hopefully, everyone in the household is willing to do his part in raising and caring for the pup. The anticipation of owning a dog often brings a lot of promises from excited family members: "I will walk him every day," "I will feed him," "I will house-train him," etc., but these things take time and effort, and promises can easily be forgotten once the novelty of the new pet has worn off.

Terrier club or perhaps an all-breed club.

Potential owners are encouraged to attend dog shows (or trials) to see the Irish Terriers in action, to meet the owners and handlers firsthand and to get an idea of what Irish Terriers look like outside a photographer's lens. Provided you approach the handlers when they are not busy with the dogs, most are more than willing to answer questions, recommend breeders and give advice.

Once you have contacted and met a few breeders and made your choice about which breeder is best suited to your needs, it's time to visit the breeder at home to see where the dogs are kept and how the pups are being raised. A good breeder will ask numerous questions to be sure you and your home will be right for an Irish. Keep in mind that many top breeders have waiting lists. Be prepared to wait for a puppy—these pups do not sit on a shelf awaiting a buyer. If you are really committed to the breeder whom you've selected, then you will wait (and hope for an early arrival!). If not, you may have to resort to your second-choice breeder. Don't be too anxious, however. If the breeder doesn't have a waiting list, or any customers, there is probably a good reason. It's no different than visiting a restaurant with no clien-

tele. The best restaurants always have waiting lists—and it's usually worth the wait. Besides, isn't a puppy more important than a fancy dinner?

When visiting the breeder, look first at the adult dogs on the premises—that's what you'll be living with for 12 to 14 years—remembering that the adults may be slightly reserved at first. They should look lean, fit and alert.

Irish Terrier litters average six to eight puppies. The puppies should be bright, friendly, outgoing and clean, with bright clear eyes, shiny black noses and correct bites (for whatever their stage of teething). All puppies in the litter should look alert and healthy. Fortunately for potential Irish Terrier owners, the breed is overall a hardy one, with no breed-specific hereditary health concerns.

The puppies may well be very dark in color, even black, as youngsters. The color will have begun to change by three months.

The puppies should have their ears glued or about to be glued. Correct ear carriage is very important in the breed; because of this, most puppies have their ears glued into the proper position commencing at ten weeks of age. It can take as long as a year for the cartilage to become firm enough to hold the ears in place. This is a job for the experienced breeder to teach the puppy buyer. Pet

Puppy ownership certainly has its ups and downs... be prepared for both!

puppies should be every bit as handsome as their show-mates!

Before you take your chosen puppy home, be sure to have a lesson in ear-setting. It's not difficult, but it is vital and must be taken down periodically to clean inside the ears, remove dead hair and old bits of glue. Since it can go on for as long as a year, it is worthwhile to pay attention!

Tails are docked and dewclaws removed at three to four days. Only a third to a quarter of the tail is docked, best gauged by an experienced breeder.

A good breeder will also start

Mom and hungry puppies. Observing the dam with the pups and watching the littermates together are good indicators of each pup's individual personality.

## PUPPY APPEARANCE

Your puppy should have a well-fed appearance but not a distended abdomen, which may indicate worms or incorrect feeding, or both. The body should be firm, with a solid feel. The skin of the abdomen should be pale pink and clean, without signs of scratching or rash. Check the legs to make certain that the breeder has had the dewclaws removed.

you off with a trimming lesson. The Irish coat is one of the easier terrier coats to keep, and stripping only needs to be done two or three times a year to remove old dead hair and bring up the lovely color of the new growth. Begin with the puppy and you will grow in expertise as the object of your endeavor grows in size.

The Irish Terrier is not considered a full adult in size until he is two to three years of age. However, he is a terrier and may retain puppyish energy throughout his entire life. A puppy is not appraised for show quality until about 10 or 12 months of age.

You should have given careful consideration to whether you want a male or a female puppy. Males tend to be slightly more assertive than the females, more prone to the "heedless, reckless pluck" side of the Irish Terrier's temperament. Bitches tend to be calmer. It does bear repeating that the Irish Terrier, particularly the male, is apt to be dog-aggressive. Intense efforts need to be made when he is a very small puppy to socialize him with friendly dogs and to persevere with obedience training. Same-sex pet ownership is definitely to be avoided. Many breeders go so far as to advise that there be only one Irish at a time in a pet home.

Breeders commonly allow visitors to see their litters by around the fifth or sixth week, and a responsible breeder will not let puppies go to new homes before they are 10 to 12 weeks of age. Breeders who permit their puppies to leave early are more interested in your money than in their puppies' well-being. By the age of 10 to 12 weeks, the pups have had time to accept the discipline meted out by their mother, making them more amenable to accepting it from humans. This "learning how to learn" process is very important. The pups also will have been handled, fed and played with to provide them with sufficient interaction with people. All of this means that when you step in to take on the puppy, much of the groundwork has been laid.

Given the long history that dogs and humans have, bonding between the two species is natural but must be nurtured. A well-bred, well-socialized Irish Terrier pup wants nothing more than to be near you and please you.

## PEDIGREE VS. REGISTRATION CERTIFICATE

Too often new owners are confused between these two important documents. Your puppy's pedigree, essentially a family tree, is a written record of a dog's genealogy of three generations or more. The pedigree will show you the names as well as performance titles of all the dogs in your pup's background. Your breeder must provide you with a registration application, with his part properly filled out. You must complete the application and send it to the AKC with the proper fee. Every puppy must come from a litter that has been AKC-registered by the breeder, born in the USA and from a sire and dam that are also registered with the AKC.

The seller must provide you with complete records to identify the puppy. The AKC requires that the seller provide the buyer with the following: breed; sex, color and markings; date of birth; litter number (when available); names and registration numbers of the parents; breeder's name; and date sold or delivered.

## COMMITMENT OF OWNERSHIP

You have chosen the Irish Terrier, which means that you have decided which characteristics you want in a dog and what type of dog will best fit into your family and lifestyle. If you have selected a breeder, you have gone a step

**PET INSURANCE**

Just like you can insure your car, your house and your own health, you likewise can insure your dog's health. Investigate a pet insurance policy by talking to your vet. Depending on the age of your dog, the breed and the kind of coverage you desire, your policy can be very affordable. Most policies cover accidental injuries, poisoning and thousands of medical problems and illnesses, including cancers. Some carriers also offer routine care and immunization coverage.

which ones are less outgoing, which ones are confident, shy, playful, friendly, aggressive, etc. Equally as important, you will learn to recognize what a healthy pup should look and act like. All of these things will help you in your search, and when you find the Irish Terrier that was meant for you, you will know it!

Researching your breed, selecting a responsible breeder and observing as many pups as possible are all important steps on the way to dog ownership. It may seem like a lot of effort...and you have not even taken the pup home yet! Remember, though, you cannot be too careful when it comes to deciding on the type of dog you want and finding out about your prospective pup's background. Buying a puppy is not—or *should* not be—just another whimsical purchase. This is one instance in which you actually *do* get to choose your own family! You may be thinking that buying a puppy should be fun—it should not be so serious and so much work. Keep in mind that your puppy is not a cuddly stuffed toy or decorative lawn ornament; rather, he is a living creature that will become a real member of your family. You will come to realize that, while buying a puppy is a pleasurable and exciting endeavor, it is not something to be taken lightly. Relax...the fun

further—you have done your research and found a responsible, conscientious person who breeds quality Irish Terriers and who should be a reliable source of help as you and your puppy adjust to life together. If you have observed a litter in action, you have obtained a firsthand look at the dynamics of a puppy "pack" and, thus, you have learned about each pup's individual personality— perhaps you have even found one that particularly appeals to you.

However, even if you have not yet found the Irish Terrier puppy of your dreams, observing pups will help you learn to recognize certain behavior and to determine what a pup's behavior indicates about his temperament. You will be able to pick out which pups are the leaders, will start when the pup comes home!

Always keep in mind that a puppy is nothing more than a baby in a furry disguise...a baby who is virtually helpless in a human world and who trusts his owner for fulfillment of his basic needs for survival. In addition to food, water and shelter, your pup needs care, protection, guidance and love. If you are not prepared to commit to this, then you are not prepared to own a dog.

"Wait a minute," you say. "How hard could this be? All of my neighbors own dogs and they seem to be doing just fine. Why should I have to worry about all of this?" Well, you should not worry about it; in fact, you will probably find that once your Irish pup gets used to his new home, he will fall into his place in the family quite naturally. However, it never hurts to emphasize the commitment of dog ownership. With some time and patience, it is really not too difficult to raise a curious and exuberant Irish Terrier pup to be a well-adjusted and well-mannered adult dog—a dog that could be your most loyal friend.

## PREPARING PUPPY'S PLACE IN YOUR HOME

Researching your breed and finding a breeder are only two aspects of the "homework" you will have

The Irish Terrier's puppy coat will change both in color and texture as he matures.

Bite of a seven-week-old. Check your chosen pup's mouth and bite. Although the bite will change somewhat as the pup grows, and minor imperfections may correct themselves, major flaws will not.

to do before taking your Irish Terrier puppy home. You will also have to prepare your home and family for the new addition. Much as you would prepare a nursery for a newborn baby, you will need to designate a place in your home that will be the puppy's own. How you prepare your home will depend on how much freedom the dog will be allowed. Whatever you decide, you must ensure that he has a place that he can "call his own."

When you take your new puppy into your home, you are bringing him into what will become his home as well. Obviously, you did not buy a puppy with the intentions of catering to his every whim and

allowing him to "rule the roost," but in order for a puppy to grow into a stable, well-adjusted dog, he has to feel comfortable in his surroundings. Remember, he is leaving the warmth and security of his mother and littermates, as well as the familiarity of the only place he has ever known, so it is important to make his transition as easy as possible. By preparing a place in your home for the puppy, you are making him feel as welcome as possible in a strange new place.

It should not take him long to get used to it, but the sudden shock of being transplanted is somewhat traumatic for a young pup. Imagine how a small child would feel in the same situation—that is how your puppy must be feeling. It is up to you to reassure him and to let him know, "Little chap, you are going to like it here!"

**YOUR SCHEDULE . . .**
If you lead an erratic, unpredictable life, with daily or weekly changes in your work requirements, consider the problems of owning a puppy. The new puppy has to be fed regularly, socialized (loved, petted, handled, introduced to other people) and, most importantly, allowed to go outdoors for house-training. As the dog gets older, he can be more tolerant of deviations in his feeding and relief schedule.

# WHAT YOU SHOULD BUY

## CRATE

To someone unfamiliar with the use of crates in dog training, it may seem like punishment to shut a dog in a crate, but this is not the case at all. More and more breeders and trainers around the world are recommending crates as preferred tools for pet puppies as well as show puppies.

Crates are not cruel—crates have many humane and highly effective uses in dog care and training. For example, crate training is a popular and very successful house-training method. In addition, a crate can keep your dog safe during travel and, perhaps most importantly, a crate provides your dog with a place of his own in your home. It serves as a "doggie bedroom" of sorts—your Irish Terrier can curl up in his crate when he wants to sleep or when he just needs a break. Many dogs sleep in their crates overnight. With soft bedding and his favorite toy, a crate becomes a cozy pseudo-den for your dog. Like his ancestors, he too will seek out the comfort and retreat of a den—you just happen to be providing him with something a little more luxurious than what his early ancestors enjoyed.

As far as purchasing a crate, the type that you buy is up to you. It will most likely be one of the two most popular types: wire or

Obtain a crate for your Irish Terrier puppy that is large enough to comfortably house the full-grown dog. A good-quality, sturdy crate can last for the dog's entire lifetime.

PHOTO COURTESY OF MIDWEST PET PRODUCTS.

fiberglass. There are advantages and disadvantages to each type. For example, a wire crate is more open, allowing the air to flow through and affording the dog a view of what is going on around him, while a fiberglass crate is sturdier. Both can double as travel crates, providing protection for the dog in the car.

The size of the crate is another thing to consider. Puppies do not stay puppies forever—in fact, sometimes it seems as if they

## CRATE-TRAINING TIPS

During crate training, you should partition off the section of the crate in which the pup stays. If he is given too big an area, this will hinder your training efforts. Crate training is based on the fact that a dog does not like to soil his sleeping quarters, so it is ineffective to keep a pup in an area that is so big that he can eliminate in one end and get far enough away from it to sleep. Also, you want to make the crate den-like for the pup. Blankets and a favorite toy will make the crate cozy for the small pup; as he grows, you may want to evict some of his "roommates" to make more room. It will take some coaxing at first, but be patient. Given some time to get used to it, your Irish will adapt to his new home-within-a-home quite nicely.

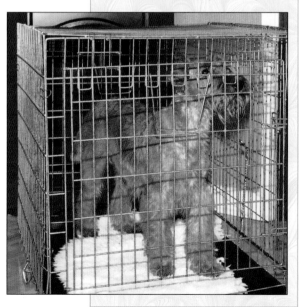

grow right before your eyes. A small crate may be fine for a young Irish Terrier pup, but it will not do him much good for long! It is better to get a crate that will accommodate your Irish both as a pup and at full size. His crate (for training, sleeping and travel) should be large enough so that the dog can lie on his side and stand up with comfort, keeping in mind the adult height at the shoulder of around 18 inches.

### BEDDING

A soft crate pad in the dog's crate will help him feel more at home, and you may also like to put a small blanket in the crate. First, these things will take the place of the leaves, twigs, etc., that the pup would use in the wild to make a den; the pup can make his own "burrow" in the crate. Although your pup is far removed from his den-making ancestors, the denning instinct is still a part of his genetic makeup. Second, until you take your pup home, he has been sleeping amid the warmth of his mother and littermates, and while a blanket is not the same as a warm, breathing body, it still provides heat and something with which to snuggle. You will want to wash your pup's bedding frequently in case he has a potty "accident" in his crate, and replace or remove anything that becomes ragged and starts to fall apart.

## TOYS

Toys are a must for dogs of all ages, especially for curious playful pups. Puppies are the "children" of the dog world, and what child does not love toys? Chew toys provide enjoyment for both dog and owner—your dog will enjoy playing with his favorite toys, while you will enjoy the fact that they distract him from chewing on your expensive shoes and leather sofa. Puppies love to chew; in fact, chewing is a physical need for pups as they are teething, and everything looks appetizing! The full range of your possessions—from old dish rag to Oriental carpet—are fair game in the eyes of a teething pup. Puppies are not all that discerning when it comes to finding something literally to "sink their teeth into"—everything tastes great!

The Irish Terrier is not among the "one-toy-fits-all" breeds. Some will play with and cherish a soft fleecy toy for life; others will destroy such an adversarial item on sight! During teething (which lasts up to a year), the dog will enjoy large hard bones and rawhides as well as hard rubber toys made especially for the teething puppy.

Use extreme caution in separating a terrier from anything it perceives to be its "possession," however, and that goes beyond his toys to things like stolen socks, a tea cozy, a new shoe, etc.

Breeders sometimes introduce their pups to crates before they leave for new homes, which is a big advantage to new owners when they set out to crate-train their puppies.

Never try to wrest it away. Instead, teach the puppy to "Give it" or "Drop it" on command. The sight of a treat in the hand facilitates negotiations!

Monitor the condition of all your pup's toys carefully and get rid of any that have been chewed to the point of becoming potentially dangerous. For example, perhaps a squeaky toy can be used as an aid in training, but is not recommended for free play. If a pup "disembowels" one of these, the small plastic squeaker inside can be dangerous if swallowed. Also be careful of natural bones, which have a tendency to splinter into sharp, dangerous pieces. Provide your Irish with safe, durable chew toys, as it takes a strong toy to withstand terrier teeth!

## LEASH

A nylon leash is probably the best option, as it is the most resistant to puppy teeth should your pup take a liking to chewing on his

## TOYS, TOYS, TOYS!

With a big variety of dog toys available, and so many that look like they would be a lot of fun for a dog, be careful in your selection. It is amazing what a set of puppy teeth can do to an innocent-looking toy; so, obviously, safety is a major consideration. Be sure to choose the most durable products that you can find. Hard nylon bones and toys are a safe bet, and many of them are offered in different scents and flavors that will be sure to capture your dog's attention. It is always fun to play a game of fetch with your dog, and there are balls and flying discs that are specially made to withstand dog teeth.

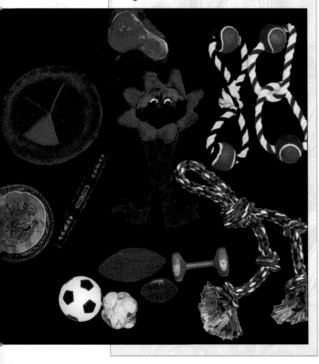

leash. Of course, this is a habit that should be nipped in the bud, but, if your pup likes to chew on his leash, he has a very slim chance of being able to chew through the strong nylon. Nylon leashes are also lightweight, which is good for a young Irish Terrier who is just getting used to the idea of walking on a leash. For everyday walking and safety purposes, the nylon leash is a good choice.

As your pup grows up and gets used to walking on the leash, you may want to purchase a flexible leash. These leashes allow you to extend the length to give the dog a broader area to explore or to shorten the length to keep the dog near you. Of course, there are leashes designed for training purposes, but these are not necessary for routine walks.

### COLLAR

Your pup should get used to wearing a collar all the time since you will want to attach his ID tags to it; plus, you have to attach the leash to something! A lightweight

## MENTAL AND DENTAL

Toys not only help your puppy get the physical and mental stimulation he needs but also provide a great way to keep his teeth clean. Hard rubber or nylon toys, especially those constructed with grooves, are designed to scrape away plaque, preventing bad breath and gum infection.

nylon collar is a good choice. Make certain that the collar fits snugly enough so that the pup cannot wriggle out of it, but is loose enough so that it will not be uncomfortably tight around the pup's neck. You should be able to fit a finger between the pup's neck and the collar. It may take some time for your pup to get used to wearing the collar, but soon he will not even notice that it is there. Choke collars are made for training, but should be used only by owners who have been instructed in exactly how to use these devices.

### FOOD AND WATER BOWLS

Your pup will need two bowls, one for food and one for water. You may want two sets of bowls, one for indoors and one for outdoors, depending on where the dog will be fed and where he will be spending time. Stainless steel or sturdy plastic bowls are popular choices. Plastic bowls are more chewable, but dogs tend not to chew on the steel variety, which

can be sterilized. It is important to buy sturdy bowls since anything is in danger of being chewed by puppy teeth and you do not want your dog to be constantly chewing apart his bowl (for his safety and for your wallet!).

### CLEANING SUPPLIES

Until a pup is house-trained, you will be doing a lot of cleaning. "Accidents" will occur, which is acceptable in the beginning stages of house-training because the puppy does not know any better. All you can do is be prepared to

Toys stimulate a pup's natural desires to play and to chew. It's best to provide them with safe toys or their energy may be used in less constructive ways.

It is your responsibility to clean up after your dog has relieved himself. Pet shops have various aids to assist in the cleanup job.

clean up any accidents as soon as they happen. Old rags or towels, paper towels, newspapers and a safe disinfectant are good to have on hand.

### BEYOND THE BASICS

The items previously discussed are the bare necessities. You will find out what else you need as you go along—grooming supplies, flea/tick protection, baby gates to partition a room, etc. These things will vary depending on your situation, but it is important that you have everything you need to feed and make your Irish Terrier comfortable in his first few days at home.

### PUPPY-PROOFING YOUR HOME

Aside from making sure that your Irish Terrier will be comfortable in your home, you also have to make sure that your home is safe for your Irish Terrier. This means taking precautions that your pup will not get into anything he should not get into and that there is nothing within his reach that may harm him should he sniff it, chew it, inspect it, etc. This probably seems obvious since, while you are primarily concerned with your pup's safety, at the same time you do not want your belongings to be ruined. Breakables should be placed out of reach if your dog is to have full run of the house. If he is to be limited to certain places within the house, keep any potentially dangerous items in the off-limits areas.

An electrical cord can pose a danger should the puppy decide to taste it—and who is going to convince a pup that it would not make a great chew toy? Cords and wires should be fastened tightly against the wall to be kept from puppy teeth. If your dog is going to spend time in a crate, make sure that there is nothing near his crate that he can reach if he sticks his curious little nose or paws through the openings. Just as you would with a child, keep all household cleaners and chemicals where the pup cannot reach them.

It is also important to make sure that the outside of your home is safe. Of course, your puppy should never be unsupervised, but a pup let loose in the yard will want to run and explore, and he should be granted that freedom. A well-maintained fence, at least 4 feet high and well-embedded into the ground, is a necessity to keep the Irish at home and safe from any neighborly indiscretions. Outdoors, the breed has a high energy level and, when not being entertained by interactive play, this "rare abandon" type of energy can lead to digging both in flower beds and under fences. Inside the home, they usually curtail this active lifestyle and behave appropriately.

Check the fence periodically to ensure that it is in good shape and make repairs as needed. Be sure to secure any gaps or weak spots in the fence. A very determined pup may return to the same spot to "work on it" until he is able to get through.

**FIRST TRIP TO THE VET**
You have selected your puppy, and your home and family are ready. Now all you have to do is collect your Irish Terrier from the breeder and the fun begins, right? Well...not so fast. Something else you need to plan is your pup's first trip to the vet. Perhaps the breeder can recommend someone in the area who specializes in terrier breeds, or maybe you know

Your puppy doesn't know that an electrical cord is dangerous; to him, it just looks like something else to chew. It is your responsibility to provide a puppy-proof environment.

some other Irish Terrier owners who can suggest a good vet. Either way, you should have an appointment arranged for your pup before you pick him up.

The pup's first visit will consist of an overall examination to make sure that the pup does not have any problems that are not apparent to you. The vet will also set up a schedule for the pup's vaccinations; the breeder will inform you of which ones the pup has already received and the vet can continue from there.

## INTRODUCTION TO THE FAMILY

Everyone in the house will be excited about the puppy's coming home and will want to pet him and play with him, but it is best to make the introductions low-key so as not to overwhelm the puppy. He is apprehensive already. It is the first time he has been separated from his mother and the breeder, and the ride to your home is likely to be the first time he has been in a car. The last

It's an exciting day when you bring your Irish Terrier puppy home from the breeder! Along with the pup, the breeder will give you the necessary papers, a diet sheet on how to feed the pup and likely a portion of the food he has been giving the pups.

thing you want to do is smother him, as this will only frighten him further. This is not to say that human contact is not extremely necessary at this stage, because this is the time when a connection between the pup and his human family is formed. Gentle petting and soothing words should help console him, as well as just putting him down and letting him explore on his own (under your watchful eye, of course).

The pup may approach the family members or may busy himself with exploring for a while. Gradually, each person should spend some time with the pup, one at a time, crouching down to get as close to the pup's level as possible, letting him sniff each person's hands and petting him gently. He definitely needs human attention and he needs to be touched—this is how to form an immediate bond. Just remember that the pup is experiencing many things for the first time, at the same time. There are new people, new noises, new smells and new things to investigate, so be gentle, be affectionate and be as comforting as you can be.

### PUP'S FIRST NIGHT HOME

You have traveled home with your new charge safely in his crate. He's been to the vet for a thorough check-up; he's been weighed, his papers have been examined and perhaps he's even been vaccinated and wormed as well. He's met the whole family, including the excited children and the less-than-happy cat. He's explored his area, his new bed, the outdoor area and anywhere else he's been permitted. He's eaten his first meal at home and relieved himself in the proper place. He's heard lots of new sounds, smelled new friends and seen more of the outside world than ever before...and that was just the first day! He's worn out and is ready for bed...or so you think!

It's puppy's first night home and you are ready to say "Good night." Keep in mind that this is his first night ever to be sleeping alone. His dam and littermates are no longer at paw's length and he's a bit scared, cold and lonely. Be reassuring to your new family member, but this is not the time to spoil him and give in to his inevitable whining.

### SKULL & CROSSBONES

Thoroughly puppy-proof your house before bringing your puppy home. Never use cockroach or rodent poisons or plant fertilizers in any area accessible to the puppy. Avoid the use of toilet cleaners. Most dogs are born with "toilet-bowl sonar" and will take a drink if the lid is left open. Also keep the trash secured and out of reach.

Puppies whine. They whine to let others know where they are and hopefully to get company out of it. Place your pup in his new bed or crate in his designated area and close the crate door. Mercifully, he may fall asleep without a peep. When the inevitable occurs, however, ignore the whining—he is fine. Be strong and keep his best interest in mind. Do not allow yourself to feel guilty and visit the pup. He will fall asleep eventually.

Many breeders recommend placing a piece of bedding from the pup's former home in his new bed so that he recognizes and is comforted by the scent of his littermates. Others still advise placing a hot water bottle in the bed for warmth. The latter may be a good idea provided the pup doesn't attempt to suckle—he'll get good and wet, and may not fall asleep so fast.

Puppy's first night can be somewhat stressful for both the

*Seven-week-old littermates snuggling up. This is what your pup will miss most during his first few nights in his new home.*

> **TRAINING TIP**
> Training your puppy takes much patience and can be frustrating at times, but you should see results from your efforts. If you have a puppy that seems untrainable, take him to a trainer or behaviorist. The dog may have a personality problem that requires the help of a professional, or perhaps you need help in learning how to train your dog.

pup and his new family. Remember that you are setting the tone of nighttime at your house. Unless you want to play with your pup every night at 10 p.m., midnight and 2 a.m., don't initiate the habit. Your family will thank you, and so will your pup!

## PREVENTING PUPPY PROBLEMS

### SOCIALIZATION

Now that you have done all of the preparatory work and have helped your pup become accustomed to his new home and family, it is about time for you to have some fun! Socializing your Irish pup gives you the opportunity to show off your new friend, and your pup gets to reap the benefits of being an adorable furry creature that people will want to pet and, in general, think is absolutely precious!

Besides getting to know his

new family, your puppy should be exposed to other people, animals and situations. This will help him become well adjusted as he grows up and less prone to being timid or fearful of the new things he will encounter. You must keep in mind that the Irish Terrier, particularly the male, is apt to be dog-aggressive. This why you must make the effort, when he is still a young pup, to socialize him with friendly dogs. Of course, he must not come into close contact with dogs you don't know well until his course of injections is fully complete.

Your pup's socialization began with the breeder, but now it is your responsibility to continue it. The socialization he receives until the age of 12 weeks is the most critical, as this is the time when he forms his impressions of the outside world. Your Irish puppy will experience a fear period

Early socialization takes place between litter-mates as they nip at and play-fight with each other, learning important lessons in the rules of the pack.

during the eight-to-ten-week-old period while he is still at the breeder's. The interaction he receives during this time should be gentle and reassuring. Lack of socialization, and/or negative experiences during the socialization period, can manifest itself in fear and aggression as the dog grows up. Your puppy needs lots of positive interaction, which of course includes human contact, affection, handling and exposure to other animals.

Once your pup has received his necessary vaccinations, feel free to take him out and about (on his leash, of course). Walk him around the neighborhood, take him on your daily errands, let people pet him, let him meet other dogs and pets, etc. Puppies do not have to try to make friends; there will be no shortage of people who will want to introduce themselves. Just make sure that you carefully supervise each meeting between your Irish and other people and pets. If the

## PUP MEETS WORLD

Thorough socialization includes not only meeting new people but also being introduced to new experiences such as riding in the car, having his coat brushed, hearing the television, walking in a crowd—the list is endless. The more your pup experiences, and the more positive the experiences are, the less of a shock and the less frightening it will be for your pup to encounter new things.

**IN DUE TIME**
It will take at least two weeks for your puppy to become accustomed to his new surroundings. Give him lots of love, attention, handling, frequent opportunities to relieve himself, a diet he likes to eat and a place he can call his own.

be comfortable around everyone. A pup that has a bad experience with a child may grow up to be a dog that is shy around or aggressive toward children.

### CONSISTENCY IN TRAINING

Dogs, being pack animals, naturally need a leader or else they try to establish dominance in their packs. When you welcome a dog into your family, the choice of who becomes the leader and who becomes the "pack" is entirely up to you! Your pup's intuitive quest for dominance, coupled with the fact that it is nearly impossible to look at an adorable Irish Terrier pup with his "puppy-dog" eyes and not cave in, give the pup an almost unfair advantage in getting the upper hand!

neighborhood children want to say hello, for example, that is great—children and pups most often make great companions. However, sometimes an excited child can unintentionally handle a pup too roughly, or an overzealous pup can playfully nip a little too hard. You want to make socialization experiences positive ones. What a pup learns during this very formative stage will affect his attitude toward future encounters. You want your dog to

A pup will definitely test the waters to see what he can and cannot do. Do not give in to those pleading eyes—stand your ground when it comes to disciplining the pup and make sure that all family members do the same. It will only confuse the pup if Mother tells him to get off the sofa when he is used to sitting up there with Father to watch the nightly news. Avoid discrepancies by having all members of the household decide on the rules before the pup even comes home...and be consistent in enforcing them! Early training shapes the dog's personality, so you cannot be unclear in what you expect.

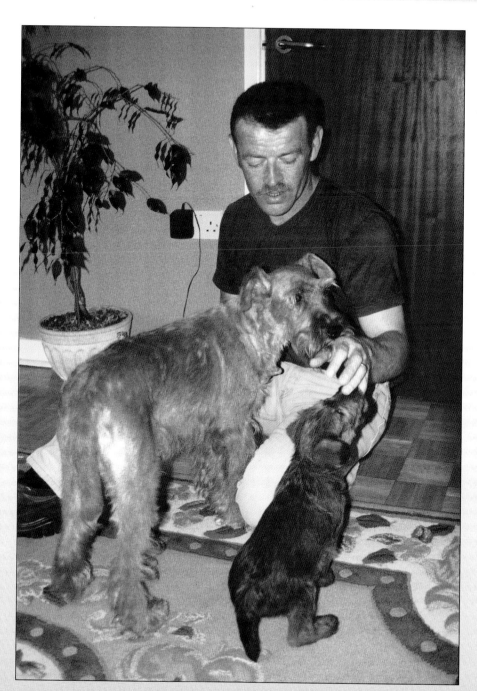

You replace the pup's dam as the leader of the pack. Are you ready for this responsibility?

## COMMON PUPPY PROBLEMS

The best way to prevent puppy problems is to be proactive in stopping an undesirable behavior as soon as it starts. The old saying "You can't teach an old dog new tricks" does not necessarily hold true, but it *is* true that it is much easier to discourage bad behavior in a young developing pup than to wait until the pup's bad behavior becomes the adult dog's bad habit. There are some problems that are especially prevalent in puppies as they develop.

### NIPPING

As puppies start to teethe, they feel the need to sink their teeth into anything available...unfortunately, that usually includes your fingers, arms, hair and toes. You may find this behavior cute for the first five seconds...until you feel just how sharp those puppy teeth are. Nipping is something you want to discourage immediately and consistently with a firm "No!" (or whatever number of firm "Nos" it takes for him to understand that you mean business). Then, replace your finger with an appropriate chew toy. While this behavior is merely annoying when the dog is young, it can become dangerous as your Irish Terrier's adult teeth grow in and his jaws develop, and he continues to think it is okay to gnaw on human appendages. Your Irish Terrier does not mean any harm with a

**PUPPY PROBLEMS**
The majority of problems that are commonly seen in young pups will disappear as your dog gets older. However, how you deal with problems when he is young will determine how he reacts to discipline as an adult dog. It is important to establish who is boss (hopefully it will be you!) right away when you are first bonding with your dog. This bond will set the tone for the rest of your life together.

friendly nip, but he also does not know the strength of his terrier teeth!

### CRYING/WHINING

Your pup will often cry, whine, whimper, howl or make some type of commotion when he is left alone. This is basically his way of calling out for attention to make sure that you know he is there and that you have not forgotten about him. Your puppy feels insecure when he is left alone, when you are out of the house and he is in his crate or when you are in another part of the house and he cannot see you. The noise he is making is an expression of the anxiety he feels at being alone, so he needs to be taught that being alone is okay. You are not actually training the dog to stop making noise; rather, you are training him to feel comfortable when he is alone and thus removing the need for him to make the noise.

This is where the crate with cozy bedding and a favorite toy comes in handy. You want to know that your pup is safe when you are not there to supervise, and you know that he will be safe in his crate rather than roaming freely about the house. In order for the pup to stay in his crate without making a fuss, he first needs to be comfortable in his crate. On that note, it is extremely important that the crate is never used as a form of punishment; this will cause the pup to view the crate as a negative place rather than as a place of his own for safety and retreat.

Accustom the pup to the crate in short, gradually increasing time intervals in which you put him in the crate, maybe with a treat, and stay in the room with him. If he cries or makes a fuss, do not go to him, but stay in his sight. Gradually he will realize that staying in his crate is okay without your help, and it will not be so traumatic for him when you are not around. You may want to leave the radio on softly when you leave the house; the sound of human voices may be comforting to him.

## CHEWING TIPS

Chewing goes hand in hand with nipping in the sense that a teething puppy is always looking for a way to soothe his aching gums. In this case, instead of chewing on you, he may have taken a liking to your favorite shoe or something else that he should not be chewing. Again, realize that this is a normal canine behavior that does not need to be discouraged, only redirected. Your pup just needs to be taught what is acceptable to chew on and what is off-limits. Consistently tell him "No!" when you catch him chewing on something forbidden and give him a chew toy.

Conversely, praise him when you catch him chewing on something appropriate. In this way, you are discouraging the inappropriate behavior and reinforcing the desired behavior. The puppy's chewing should stop after his adult teeth have come in, but an adult dog continues to chew for various reasons—perhaps because he is bored, needs to relieve tension or just likes to chew. That is why it is important to redirect his chewing when he is still young.

## DIETARY AND FEEDING CONSIDERATIONS

Today the choices of food for your Irish Terrier are many and varied. There are simply dozens of brands of food in all sorts of flavors and textures, ranging from puppy diets to those for seniors. There are even hypoallergenic and low-calorie diets available. Because your Irish Terrier's food has a bearing on coat, health and temperament, it is essential that the most suitable diet is selected for an Irish Terrier of his age. It is fair to say, however, that even experienced owners can be perplexed by the enormous range of foods available. Only understanding what is best for your dog will help you reach an informed decision.

Dog foods are produced in three basic types: dry, semi-moist and canned. Dry foods are useful for the cost-conscious, for overall they tend to be less expensive than semi-moist or canned foods. Dry foods also contain the least fat and the most preservatives. In general, canned foods are made up of 60–70% water, while semi-moist ones often contain so much sugar that they are perhaps the least preferred by owners, even though their dogs seem to like them.

When selecting your dog's diet, three stages of development

### STORING DOG FOOD

You must store your dry dog food carefully. Open packages of dog food quickly lose their vitamin value, usually within 90 days of being opened. Mold spores and vermin could also contaminate the food.

## FOOD PREFERENCE

Selecting the best dry dog food is difficult. There is no majority consensus among veterinary scientists as to the value of nutrient analysis (protein, fat, fiber, moisture, ash, cholesterol, minerals, etc.). All agree that feeding trials are what matter most, but you also have to consider the individual dog. The dog's weight, age and activity level, and what pleases his taste, all must be considered. It is probably best to take the advice of your vet. Every dog's dietary requirements vary, even during the lifetime of a particular dog.

If your dog is fed a good dry food, he does not require supplements of meat or vegetables. Dogs do appreciate a little variety in their diets, so you may choose to stay with the same brand but vary the flavor. Alternatively, you may wish to add a little flavored stock to give a difference to the taste.

them on the nipples, having selected ones with plenty of milk. This early milk supply is important in providing the essential colostrum, which protects the puppies during the first eight to ten weeks of their lives. Although a mother's milk is much better than any commercially prepared milk formula, despite there being some excellent ones available, if the puppies do not feed, the breeder will have to feed them by hand. For those with less experience, advice from a vet is important so that not only the right quantity of milk is fed but also that of correct quality, fed at suitably frequent intervals, usually every two hours during the first few days of life.

Puppies should be allowed to nurse from their mothers for about the first six weeks, although, starting around the third or fourth week, the breeder will begin to introduce small portions of suit-

The puppy diet is very important in promoting proper growth and development. Your breeder knows which foods work best with his own dogs and will be an invaluable source of advice as your pup grows.

must be considered: the puppy stage, the adult stage and the senior stage.

### PUPPY STAGE

Puppies instinctively want to suck milk from their mother's teats; a normal puppy will exhibit this behavior just a few moments following birth. If puppies do not attempt to suckle within the first half-hour or so, they should be encouraged to do so by placing

One-week-old
puppies, nursing.
Pups get all of
the nutrition they
need, plus
protection from
disease, while
nursing from
their mother.

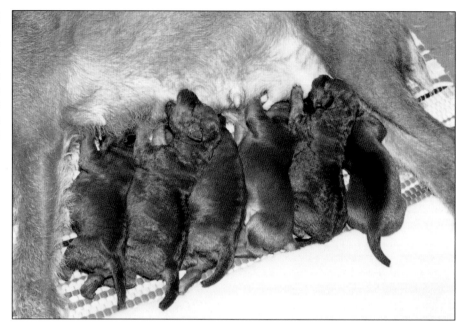

able solid food. Most breeders like to introduce alternate milk and meat meals initially, building up to weaning time.

By the time the puppies are seven or a maximum of eight weeks old, they should be fully weaned and fed solely on a proprietary puppy food. Selection of the most suitable, good-quality diet at this time is essential, for a puppy's fastest growth rate is during the first year of life. Vets and breeders are able to offer advice in this regard. The frequency of meals will be reduced over time, and it is recommended that a puppy be changed to adult food at about two years of age. Puppy and junior diets should be well

balanced for the needs of your dog so that, except in certain circumstances, additional vitamins, minerals and proteins will not be required.

**ADULT DIETS**
A dog is considered an adult when it has stopped growing. The Irish Terrier is not considered a full adult in size until he is two to three years of age, and it is recommended to keep the Irish on a puppy diet until around two years of age. Again you should rely upon your vet or breeder to recommend an acceptable maintenance diet. Major dog-food manufacturers specialize in this type of food, and it is merely necessary for you to select the one best

suited to your dog's needs. Active dogs have different requirements than sedate dogs.

### SENIOR DIETS

As dogs get older, their metabolism changes. The older dog usually exercises less, moves more slowly and sleeps more. This change in lifestyle and physiological performance requires a change in diet. Since these changes take place slowly, they might not be recognizable. What is easily recognizable is weight gain. By continuing to feed your dog an adult-maintenance diet when he is slowing down metabolically, your dog will gain weight. Obesity in an older dog compounds the health problems that already accompany old age.

As your dog gets older, few of his organs function up to par. The kidneys slow down and the intestines become less efficient. These age-related factors are best handled with a change in diet and a change in feeding schedule to give smaller portions that are more easily digested. After beginning with the adult diet at around the age of two, your Irish will remain on the adult-maintenance diet for another six to eight years before shifting to a senior food. Dogs mature individually. A dog given daily vigorous exercise will not show his age as early as will a dog permitted to sleep all day and watch the TV in the evening.

There is no single best diet for every older dog. While many dogs do well on light or senior diets, other dogs do better on puppy diets or other special premium

### GRAIN-BASED DIETS

Some less expensive dog foods are based on grains and other plant proteins. While these products may appear to be attractively priced, many breeders prefer a diet based on animal proteins and believe that they are more conducive to your dog's health. Many grain-based diets rely on soy protein, which may cause flatulence (passing gas).

There are many cases, however, when your dog might require a special diet. These special requirements should only be recommended by your vet.

## DRINK, DRANK, DRUNK— MAKE IT A DOUBLE

In both humans and dogs, as well as other living organisms, water forms the major part of nearly every body tissue. Naturally, we take water for granted, but, without it, life as we know it would cease.

For dogs, water is needed to keep their bodies functioning biochemically. Additionally, water is needed to replace the water lost while panting. Unlike humans, who are able to sweat to dissipate heat, dogs must pant to cool down, thereby losing the vital water that their bodies need to regulate their body temperatures. Humans lose electrolyte-containing products and other body-fluid components through sweating; dogs do not lose anything except water.

Water is essential always, but especially so when the weather is hot or humid or when your dog is exercising or working vigorously.

diets such as lamb and rice. Be sensitive to your senior Irish Terrier's diet, as this will help control other problems that may arise with your old friend.

## WATER

Just as your dog needs proper nutrition from his food, water is an essential "nutrient" as well. Water keeps the dog's body properly hydrated and promotes normal function of the body's systems. While you are housetraining your Irish Terrier, it is necessary to keep an eye on how much water your puppy is drinking, but, once he is reliably trained, he should have access to clean fresh water at all times, especially if you feed dry food only. Make certain that the dog's water bowl is clean, and change the water often.

## EXERCISE

All dogs require some form of exercise, regardless of breed, and the Irish Terrier will enjoy almost as much exercise as you can give him. A sedentary lifestyle is as harmful to a dog as it is to a person. Although the Irish is a fairly active breed that enjoys exercise, you don't have to be an Olympic athlete to provide your dog with a sufficient amount of activity! Exercising your Irish Terrier can be enjoyable and healthy for both of you. On-leash walks, once the puppy reaches three or four months of age, will stimulate heart rates and build muscle for both dog and owner. As the dog reaches adulthood, the speed and distance of the walks can be increased as long as they are both kept reasonable and comfortable for both of you.

Keep in mind that it is wise to avoid strenuous exercise—be it walking or playing—until the pup has physically matured. This is both to avoid stress to his growing frame and to avoid temperament problems. This is a breed that does everything but sleep with rare abandon. A physically over-stimulated Irish may become too fiery in temperament, something you do not want to encourage in a youngster.

Play sessions in the yard and letting the dog run free in a fenced area under your supervision also are sufficient forms of exercise for the Irish Terrier. Fetching games can be played indoors or out; these are excellent for giving your dog active play that he will enjoy. Chasing things that move comes naturally to dogs of all breeds. When your Irish Terrier runs after the ball or object, praise him for picking it up and encourage him to bring it back to you for another throw. Never go to the object and pick it up yourself, or you'll soon find that you are the one retrieving the objects rather than the dog! If you choose to play games outdoors, you must have a securely

**WALKING LIKE A PRO**
For many people, it is difficult to imagine putting their dog's well-being in someone else's hands, but, if you are unable to give your dog his necessary exercise breaks, hiring a professional dog walker may be a good idea. Dog walkers offer your dog exercise, a chance to work off energy and companionship—all things that keep him healthy. Seek referrals from your vet, breeder or groomer to find a reputable dog walker.

fenced-in yard and/or have the dog attached to at least a 25-foot light line for security. You want your Irish Terrier to run, but not run away!

If you have the means, the Irish is still capable of being an all-around farm dog or hunter. Given either job, he will make a good show of it and get plenty of exercise.

Bear in mind that an overweight dog should never be suddenly over-exercised; instead, he should be encouraged to increase exercise slowly. And remember, not only is exercise essential to keep the dog's body fit, it is essential to his mental well-being. A bored dog will find something to do, which often manifests itself in some type of destructive behavior. In this sense, exercise is essential for the owner's mental well-being as well!

An Irish Terrier before being groomed. The best way to groom is with the dog standing securely on a sturdy grooming table at an easy-to-work-with height.

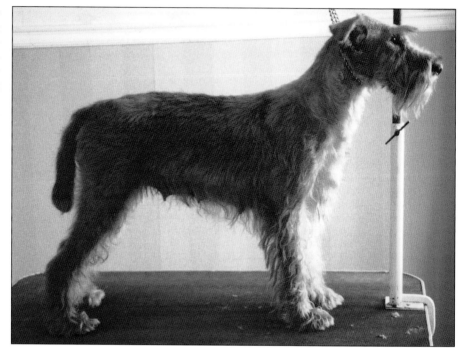

## GROOMING

All grooming should take place with the dog up on a table with firm footing (a mat or towel) and a noose, attached to the ceiling or to a hook above the table, to hold his head steady. Begin when your Irish is a puppy by stroking him, petting him, touching his toes and ears, opening his mouth—all done gently, while keeping in mind that grooming sessions are not play-time (he will try to convince you otherwise). Gradually introduce brushing and nail clipping or filing. Irish Terriers seem to have a distinct preference for having their nails filed. Regular brushing twice a week will rid the coat of debris and dead hair and also stimulate the natural oils in the skin.

Plucking (or stripping) is the preferred method for working the coat and is not difficult to learn. Pin up a photograph of a well-trimmed show dog as a guide. Begin by brushing the dog out. Then grasp a few long hairs between your thumb and finger and use a quick, firm but gentle jerk in the direction that the hairs grow. Use a stripping knife after you have practiced with your fingers. Remove the long hair from the neck, back, sides, quarters and tail. Some hair is left on the legs, but pull out the long light hairs.

Scissor the hair around the feet and between the footpads. Remove all of the long hair on the top and sides of the head so it looks smooth, but leave some eyebrows. Tidy up the whiskers, leaving a short beard. If this whole procedure sounds like too much work, either get out the clippers or find a groomer to groom your Irish for you. Clipping has two drawbacks—it will soften the coat and lighten its color.

Regular brushing and grooming eliminate the need for baths. Frequently bathing the Irish ruins the coat, which should be hard and wiry and shed water. Bathing can also dry the skin, causing itching and scratching. This is a low-maintenance terrier.

## GROOMING EQUIPMENT

How much grooming equipment you purchase will depend on how much grooming you are going to do. Here are some basics:

- Grooming table
- Natural bristle brush
- Slicker brush
- Metal comb
- Scissors
- Stripping knife
- Electric clippers (optional)
- Ear cleaner
- Cotton balls
- Towels
- Nail clippers

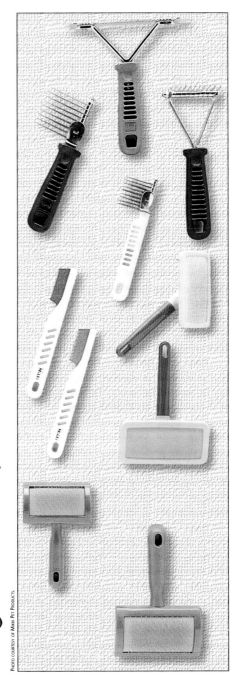

Your local pet shop should have the tools necessary to properly groom your Irish Terrier.

PHOTO COURTESY OF MIKKI PET PRODUCTS.

This Irish puppy is looking good as he strikes a confident pose on the grooming table.

You may need to practice with the stripping knife a few times before you get it right.

### Ear Cleaning

The ears should be kept clean with a cotton ball and ear powder made especially for dogs. Do not probe into the ear canal with a cotton swab, as this can cause injury. Be on the lookout for any signs of infection or ear-mite infestation. If your Irish Terrier has been shaking his head or scratching at his ears frequently, this usually indicates a problem. If the dog's ears have an unusual odor, this is a sure sign of mite infestation or infection, and a signal to have his ears checked by the vet.

Brushing the puppy with a rubber brush.

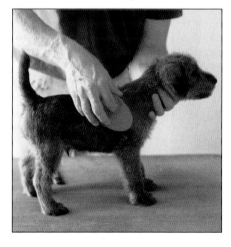

### Nail Clipping

Your Irish Terrier should be accustomed to having his nails trimmed or filed at an early age, since nail maintenance will be part of your grooming routine throughout his life. A dog's long nails can scratch someone unintentionally, and they also have a better chance of ripping and bleeding, or causing the feet to spread. A good rule of thumb is that if you can hear your dog's nails' clicking on the floor when he walks, his nails are too long.

Before you start cutting, make sure you can identify the "quick" in each nail. The quick is a blood vessel that runs through the center of each nail and grows rather close to the end. The quick will bleed if accidentally cut, which will be quite painful for the dog as it contains nerve endings. Keep some type of clotting agent on hand, such as a styptic pencil or styptic powder (the type used for shaving). This will stop the bleeding quickly when applied to the end of the nail. Do not panic if you cut the quick, just stop the bleeding and talk soothingly to your dog. Once he has calmed down, move on to the next nail. It is better to clip or file a little at a time, particularly with black-nailed dogs.

Hold your pup steady as you begin working on his nails; you do not want him to make any sudden movements or run away. Talk to him soothingly and stroke him. If using a clipper, hold his foot in your hand and simply take off the end of each nail with one

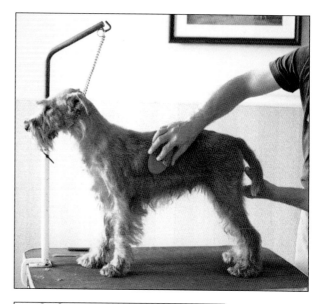

Above: A rubber brush can be used to give the adult's coat a once-over.

Left: Stripping gives the adult coat the proper hard, wiry texture.

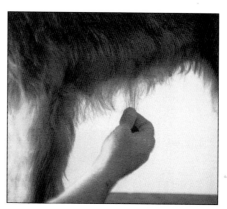

Hand plucking means that you pluck dead hair by firmly grasping it between your thumb and forefinger and pulling it out. This is painless for the dog when done correctly.

The characteristic facial furnishings need attention, too. They are gently brushed forward, toward the nose.

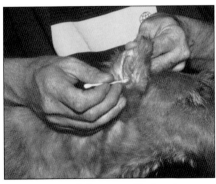

Clean the area around the eyes gently. It is probably safer to use a cotton ball to avoid poking the dog if he should suddenly move his head.

Trimming the hair between the footpads gives a neater-looking foot, plus prevents excess hair from building up and causing discomfort to the dog.

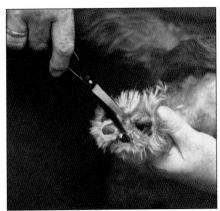

Clean the ears regularly, never probing into the ear canal or delving more deeply than you can see.

Enlisting the help of a friend can make grooming easier.

Some Irish Terriers prefer to have their nails filed rather than clipped, but whatever method that you choose, start when your dog is young and he should grow up being tolerant of the procedure.

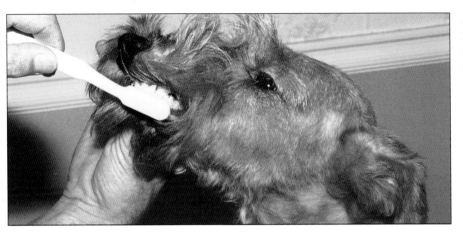

Make brushing your Irish's teeth part of your grooming routine.

swift clip. If filing, hold his foot and file down each nail, being careful not to get too close to the quick. You should purchase tools that are made for use on dogs; you can probably find files and nail clippers wherever you buy pet supplies.

## TRAVELING WITH YOUR DOG

### CAR TRAVEL
You should accustom your Irish Terrier to riding in a car at an early age. You may or may not take him in the car often, but at the very least he will need to go to the vet and you do not want these trips to be traumatic for the dog or troublesome for you. The safest way for a dog to ride in the car is in his crate. If he uses a crate in the house, you can use the same crate for travel.

Put the pup in the crate and see how he reacts. If he seems uneasy, you can have a passenger hold him on his lap while you drive. Another option for car travel is a specially made safety harness for dogs, which straps the dog in much like a seat belt. Do not let the dog roam loose in the vehicle—this is very dangerous! If you should stop short, your dog can be thrown and injured. If the dog starts climbing on you and pestering you while you are driving, you will not be able to concentrate on the road. It is an unsafe situation for everyone—human and canine.

For long trips, be prepared to stop to let the dog relieve himself. Take with you whatever you need to clean up after him, including some paper towels and perhaps some old bath towels for use should he have a potty accident in the car or become carsick.

### AIR TRAVEL
Contact your chosen airline well in advance before proceeding with

**TRAVELING ABROAD**

For international travel you will have to make arrangements well in advance (perhaps months), as countries' regulations pertaining to bringing in animals differ. There may be special health certificates and/or vaccinations that your dog will need before taking the trip; sometimes this has to be done within a certain time frame. In rabies-free countries, you will need to bring proof of the dog's rabies vaccination and there may be a quarantine period upon arrival.

case a light meal is best. For long trips, you will have to attach food and water bowls to the dog's crate so that airline employees can tend to him between legs of the trip.

Make sure that your dog is properly identified and that your contact information appears on his ID tags and on his crate. Your Irish Terrier will travel in a different area of the plane than the human passengers, so every rule must be strictly followed to prevent the slight risk of getting separated from your dog.

### VACATIONS AND BOARDING

So you want to take a family vacation—and you want to include *all* members of the family. You would probably make arrangements for accommodations ahead of time anyway, but this is especially important when traveling with a dog. You do not want to make an overnight stop at the only place around for miles, only to find out that they do not allow dogs. Also, you do not want to reserve a place for your family without confirming that you are traveling with a dog, because, if it is against the hotel's policy, you may end up without a place to stay.

your travel plans that include your Irish Terrier. Summer vacations may be difficult, as airlines often will not transport pets as checked baggage during the summer months to avoid heat-related problems. Dogs are required to travel in a fiberglass crate and you should always check in advance with the airline regarding specific requirements for the crate's size, type and labeling. If your dog's crate does not fall within the airline's specifications, you are usually able to obtain a crate from the airline.

To help put the dog at ease, give him one of his favorite toys in the crate. Do not feed the dog for several hours prior to checking in so that you minimize his need to relieve himself. However, some airlines require that the dog must be fed within a certain time frame of arriving at the airport; in any

Alternatively, if you are traveling and choose not to bring your Irish Terrier, you will have to make arrangements for him while you are away. Some options are to take him to a neighbor's house to stay while you are gone, to have a trusted neighbor come by often or stay at your house or to bring your dog to a reputable boarding kennel. If you choose to board him at a kennel, you should visit in advance to see the facilities provided and where the dogs are kept. Are the dogs' areas spacious and kept clean? Talk to some of the employees and observe how they treat the dogs—do they spend time with the dogs, play with them, exercise them, etc.? Do they have experience with terriers? Also find out the kennel's policy on vaccinations and what they require. This is for all of the dogs' safety, since there is a greater risk of diseases being passed from dog to dog when dogs are kept together.

## IDENTIFICATION

Your Irish Terrier is your valued companion and friend. That is why you always keep a close eye on him and you have made sure that he cannot escape from the yard or wriggle out of his collar and run away from you. However, accidents can happen and there may come a time when your dog unexpectedly becomes separated from you. If this unfortunate event should occur, the first thing on your mind will be finding him. Proper identification, including an ID tag, and possibly a tattoo and/or a microchip, will increase the chances of his being returned to you safely and quickly.

## IDENTIFICATION OPTIONS

As puppies become more and more expensive, especially those puppies of high quality for showing and/or breeding, they have a greater chance of being stolen. The usual collar dog tag is, of course, easily removed. But there are two more permanent techniques that have become widely used for identification.

The puppy microchip implantation involves the injection of a small microchip, about the size of a corn kernel, under the skin of the dog. If your dog shows up at a clinic or shelter, or is offered for resale under less-than-savory circumstances, he can be positively identified by the microchip. The microchip is scanned, and a registry quickly identifies you as the owner.

Tattooing is done on various parts of the dog, from his belly to his ears. The number tattooed can be your telephone number, the dog's registration number or any other number that you can easily memorize. When professional dog thieves see a tattooed dog, they usually lose interest. For the safety of our dogs, no laboratory facility or dog broker will accept a tattooed dog as stock.

Discuss microchipping and tattooing with your vet and breeder. Some vets perform these services on their own premises for a reasonable fee. To ensure the effectiveness of your dog's ID, be certain that the dog is then properly registered with a legitimate national database.

# TRAINING YOUR
# IRISH TERRIER

Living with an untrained dog is a lot like owning a piano that you do not know how to play—it is a nice object to look at, but it does not do much more than that to bring you pleasure. Now try taking piano lessons, and suddenly the piano comes alive and brings forth magical sounds and rhythms that set your heart singing and your body swaying.

The same is true with your Irish Terrier. Any dog is a big responsibility and, if not trained sensibly, may develop unacceptable behavior that annoys you or could even cause family friction.

To train your Irish Terrier, you may like to enroll in an obedience class. Teach your dog good manners as you learn how and why he behaves the way he does. Find out how to communicate with your dog and how to recognize and understand his communications with you. Suddenly the dog takes on a new role in your life—he is clever, interesting, well behaved and fun to be with. He demonstrates his bond of devotion to you daily. In other words, your Irish Terrier does wonders for your ego because he constantly

## PARENTAL GUIDANCE

Training a dog is a life experience. Many parents admit that much of what they know about raising children they learned from caring for their dogs. Dogs respond to love, fairness and guidance, just as children do. Become a good dog owner and you may become an even better parent.

reminds you that you are not only his leader, you are his hero!

Those involved with teaching dog obedience and counseling owners about their dogs' behavior have discovered some interesting facts about dog ownership. For example, training dogs when they are puppies results in the highest rate of success in developing well-mannered and well-adjusted adult dogs. Training an older dog, from six months to six years of age, can produce almost equal results, providing that the owner accepts the dog's slower rate of learning capability and is willing to work patiently to help the dog succeed at developing to his fullest potential. Unfortunately, many owners of untrained adult dogs lack the patience factor, so they do not persist until their dogs are successful at learning particular behaviors.

Training a puppy aged 10 to 16 weeks (20 weeks at the most) is like working with a dry sponge in a pool of water. The pup soaks up whatever you show him and constantly looks for more things to do and learn. At this early age, his body is not yet producing hormones, and therein lies the reason for such a high rate of success. Without hormones, he is focused on his owners and not particularly interested in investigating other places, dogs, people, etc. You are his leader: his provider of food, water, shelter and security. He latches onto you and wants to stay close. He will usually follow you from room to room, will not let you out of his sight when you are outdoors with him and will respond in like manner to the people and animals you encounter. If you greet a friend warmly, he will be happy to greet the person as well. If, however, you are hesitant or anxious about the approach of a stranger, he will respond accordingly.

Once the puppy begins to

Your Irish Terrier puppy is an alert and able learner, ready to soak up the lessons you teach him.

## MEALTIME

Mealtime should be a peaceful time for your puppy. Do not put his food and water bowls in a high-traffic area in the house. For example, give him his own little corner of the kitchen where he can eat undisturbed and where he will not be underfoot. Do not allow small children or other family members to disturb the pup when he is eating.

produce hormones, his natural curiosity emerges and he begins to investigate the world around him. It is at this time when you may notice that the untrained dog begins to wander away from you and even ignore your commands to stay close. When this behavior becomes a problem, you have two choices: get rid of the dog or train him. It is strongly urged that you choose the latter option.

You usually will be able to find obedience classes within a reasonable distance from your home, but you can also do a lot to train your dog yourself. Sometimes there are classes available, but the tuition is too costly. Whatever the circumstances, the solution to training your dog without formal obedience classes lies within the pages of this book.

This chapter is devoted to helping you train your Irish Terrier at home. If the recommended procedures are followed faithfully, you may expect positive results that will prove rewarding both to you and your dog.

Whether your new charge is a puppy or a mature adult, the methods of teaching and the techniques we use in training basic behaviors are the same. After all, no dog, whether puppy or adult, likes harsh or inhumane methods. All creatures, however, respond favorably to gentle motivational methods and sincere praise and encouragement. Now let us get started.

## HOUSE-TRAINING

You can train a puppy to relieve himself wherever you choose, but this must be somewhere suitable. You should bear in mind from the outset that when your puppy is old enough to go out in public places, any canine deposits must be removed at once. You will always have to carry with you a small plastic bag or "poop-scoop."

Outdoor training includes such surfaces as grass, soil and cement. Indoor training usually means training your dog to newspaper. When deciding on the surface and location that you will want your Irish Terrier to use, be sure it is going to be permanent. Training your dog to grass and then changing your mind a few months later is extremely difficult for both dog and owner.

Next, choose the command you will use each and every time you want your puppy to void. "Hurry up" and "Let's go" are examples of commands commonly used by dog owners. Get in the habit of giving the puppy your chosen relief command before you take him out. That way, when he becomes an adult, you will be able to determine if he wants to go out when you ask him. A confirmation will be signs of interest such as wagging his tail, watching you intently, going to the door, etc.

## CALM DOWN

Dogs will do anything for your attention. If you reward the dog when he is calm and attentive, you will develop a well-mannered dog. If, on the other hand, you greet your dog excitedly and encourage him to wrestle with you, the dog will greet you the same way and you will have a hyperactive dog on your hands.

### PUPPY'S NEEDS

Your puppy needs to relieve himself after play periods, after each meal, after he has been sleeping and at any time he indicates that he is looking for a place to urinate or defecate. The urinary and intestinal tract muscles of very young puppies are not fully developed. Therefore, like human babies, puppies need to relieve themselves frequently.

Take your puppy out often— every hour for a ten-week-old, for example—and always immediately after sleeping and eating. The older the puppy, the less often he will need to relieve himself. Finally, as a mature healthy adult, he will require only three to five relief trips per day.

### HOUSING

Since the types of housing and control you provide for your puppy have a direct relationship on the success of house-training,

If you have a fenced-in yard, pick an out-of-the way spot for your Irish's relief site and train him to use it by leading him there on his leash. In a short time, he will learn to locate the area on his own.

we consider the various aspects of both before we begin training.

Taking a new puppy home and turning him loose in your house can be compared to turning a child loose in a sports arena and telling the child that the place is all his! The sheer enormity of the place would be too much for him to handle. Instead, offer the puppy clearly defined areas where he can play, sleep, eat and live. A room of the house where the family gathers is the most obvious

Your dog's schedule for house-training begins with puppyhood and continues for your Irish's whole life.

**KEEP SMILING**
Never train your dog, puppy or adult, when you are angry or in a sour mood. Dogs are very sensitive to human feelings, especially anger, and if your dog senses that you are angry or upset, he will connect your anger with his training and learn to resent or fear his training sessions.

choice. Puppies are social animals and need to feel a part of the pack right from the start. Hearing your voice, watching you while you are doing things and smelling you nearby are all positive reinforcers that he is now a member of your pack. Usually a family room, the kitchen or a nearby adjoining breakfast area is ideal for providing safety and security for both puppy and owner.

Within the designated room, there should be a smaller area that the puppy can call his own. An alcove, a wire or fiberglass dog crate or a partitioned (not boarded!) corner from which he can view the activities of his new family will be fine. The size of the area or crate is the key factor here. The area must be large enough so that the puppy can lie down and stretch out, as well as stand up, without rubbing his head on the top. At the same time, it must be small enough so that he cannot relieve himself at one end and sleep at the other without coming

# Canine Development Schedule

It is important to understand how and at what age a puppy develops into adulthood. If you are a puppy owner, consult the following Canine Development Schedule to determine the stage of development your Irish puppy is currently experiencing. This knowledge will help you as you work with the puppy in the weeks and months ahead.

| Period | Age | Characteristics |
|---|---|---|
| **FIRST TO THIRD** | **BIRTH TO SEVEN WEEKS** | Puppy needs food, sleep and warmth, and responds to simple and gentle touching. Needs mother for security and disciplining. Needs littermates for learning and interacting with other dogs. Pup learns to function within a pack and learns pack order of dominance. Begin socializing with adults and children for short periods. Begins to become aware of his environment. |
| **FOURTH** | **EIGHT TO TWELVE WEEKS** | Brain is fully developed. Needs socializing with outside world. Remove from mother and littermates. Needs to change from canine pack to human pack. Human dominance necessary. Fear period occurs between 8 and 16 weeks. Avoid fright and pain. |
| **FIFTH** | **THIRTEEN TO SIXTEEN WEEKS** | Training and formal obedience should begin. Less association with other dogs, more with people, places, situations. Period will pass easily if you remember this is pup's change-to-adolescence time. Be firm and fair. Flight instinct prominent. Permissiveness and over-disciplining can do permanent damage. Praise for good behavior. |
| **JUVENILE** | **FOUR TO EIGHT MONTHS** | Another fear period about 7 to 8 months of age. It passes quickly, but be cautious of fright and pain. Sexual maturity reached. Dominant traits established. Dog should understand sit, down, come and stay by now. |

NOTE: THESE ARE APPROXIMATE TIME FRAMES. ALLOW FOR INDIVIDUAL DIFFERENCES IN PUPPIES.

**PAPER CAPER**
Never line your pup's sleeping area with newspaper. Puppy litters are usually raised on newspaper and, once in your home, the puppy will immediately associate newspaper with voiding. Never put newspaper on any floor while house-training, as this will only confuse the puppy. If you are paper-training him, use paper in his designated relief area only. Finally, restrict water intake after evening meals. Offer a few licks at a time—never let a young puppy gulp water after meals.

into contact with his droppings before he is fully trained to relieve himself outside. Dogs are, by nature, clean animals and will not remain close to their relief areas unless forced to do so. In those cases, they then become dirty dogs and usually remain that way for life.

The dog's designated area should contain clean bedding and a toy. Water should always be available to your Irish Terrier, but avoid putting water or food in his crate until house-training has been accomplished. Drinking and eating will activate his digestive processes and ultimately defeat your purpose in training, as well as make the puppy very uncomfortable as he attempts to "hold it."

**Paper-training is fine for very young pups, but do you want to deal with an adult's relieving himself indoors? It's best to start training your Irish to "go" outdoors from day one.**

## CONTROL

By *control*, we mean helping the puppy to create a lifestyle pattern that will be compatible to that of his human pack (YOU!). Just as we guide little children to learn our way of life, we must show the puppy when it is time to play, eat, sleep, exercise and even entertain himself.

Your puppy should always sleep in his crate. He should also learn that, during times of household confusion and excessive human activity, such as at breakfast when family members are preparing for the day, he can play by himself in relative safety and comfort in his designated area. Each time you leave the puppy alone, he should understand exactly where he is to stay.

Puppies are chewers and cannot tell the difference between things that are safe to chew on and inappropriate items like lamp cords, television wires, shoes, table legs, etc. Chewing into a television wire, for example, can be fatal to the puppy, while a shorted wire can start a fire in the house. If the puppy chews on the arm of the chair when he is alone, you will probably discipline him angrily when you get home. Thus, he makes the association that your coming home means he is going to be punished. (He will not remember chewing the chair and is incapable of making the association of the discipline with his naughty

**FAMILY TIES**
If you have other pets in the home and/or interact often with the pets of friends and other family members, your pup will respond to those pets in much the same manner as you do. It is only when you show fear of or resentment toward another animal that he will act fearful or unfriendly.

deed.) Accustoming the pup to his designated area not only keeps him safe but also avoids his engaging in destructive behaviors when you are not around.

Times of excitement and more than nomral activity, such as special occasions, family parties, etc., can be fun for the puppy, providing that he can view the activities from the security of his crate or designated area. He is not underfoot and he is not being fed all sorts of tidbits that will probably cause him stomach distress, yet he still feels a part of the fun.

### ESTABLISHING A HOUSE-TRAINING SCHEDULE

A puppy should be taken to his relief area each time he is released from his designated area, after meals, after play sessions and when he first awakens in the morning (at age ten weeks, this can mean 5 a.m.!). The puppy will indicate that he's ready "to go" by circling or sniffing busily— do not misinterpret these signs. For a puppy around ten weeks of age, a routine of taking him out every hour is necessary. As the puppy grows, he will be able to wait for longer periods of time.

Keep trips to his relief area short. Stay no more than five or six minutes and then return to the house. If he goes during that time, praise him lavishly and take him indoors immediately. If he does not, but he has an accident when you go back indoors, pick him up immediately, say "No! No!" and return to his relief area. Wait a few minutes, then return to the house again. Never hit a puppy or put his face in urine or excrement when he has had an accident!

Once indoors, put the puppy in his crate until you have had time to clean up his accident. Then, release him to the family area and watch him more closely than before. Chances are, his accident was a result of your not picking up his signal or waiting too long before offering him the opportunity to relieve himself. Never hold a grudge against the puppy for accidents.

Let the puppy learn that going outdoors means it is time to relieve himself, not to play. Once trained, he will be able to play indoors and out and still differentiate between the times for play versus the times for relief. Help him develop regular hours for naps, being alone, playing by himself and just resting, all in his crate. Encourage him to entertain himself while you are busy with your activities. Let him learn that having you near is comforting, but it is not your main purpose in life to provide him with undivided attention.

Each time you put your puppy in his own area, use the same command, whatever suits best. Soon he will run to his crate or special area when he hears you say those words.

Crate training provides safety

### HOW MANY TIMES A DAY?

| AGE | RELIEF TRIPS |
| --- | --- |
| To 14 weeks | 10 |
| 14–22 weeks | 8 |
| 22–32 weeks | 6 |
| Adulthood | 4 |
| (dog stops growing) | |

These are estimates, of course, but they are a guide to the *minimum* number of opportunities a dog should have each day to relieve himself.

for you, the puppy and the home. It also provides the puppy with a feeling of security, and that helps the puppy achieve self-confidence and clean habits. Remember that one of the primary ingredients in house-training your puppy is control. Regardless of your lifestyle, there will always be occasions when you will need to have a place where your dog can stay and be happy and safe. Crate training is the answer for now and in the future.

In conclusion, a few key elements are really all you need for a successful house-training method—consistency, frequency,

# THE SUCCESS METHOD

Success that comes by luck is usually short-lived. Success that comes by well-thought-out proven methods is often more easily achieved and permanent. This is the Success Method. It is designed to give you, the puppy owner, a simple yet proven way to help your puppy develop clean living habits and a feeling of security in his new environment.

## 6 Steps to Successful Crate Training

**1** Tell the puppy "Crate time!" and place him in the crate with a small treat (a piece of cheese or half of a biscuit). Let him stay in the crate for five minutes while you are in the same room. Then release him and praise lavishly. Never release him when he is fussing. Wait until he is quiet before you let him out.

**2** Repeat Step 1 several times a day.

**3** The next day, place the puppy in the crate as before. Let him stay there for ten minutes. Do this several times.

**4** Continue building time in five-minute increments until the puppy stays in his crate for 30 minutes with you in the room. Always take him to his relief area after prolonged periods in his crate.

**5** Now go back to Step 1 and let the puppy stay in his crate for five minutes, this time while you are out of the room.

**6** Once again, build crate time in five-minute increments with you out of the room. When the puppy will stay willingly in his crate (he may even fall asleep!) for 30 minutes with you out of the room, he will be ready to stay in it for several hours at a time.

praise, control and supervision. By following these procedures with a normal, healthy puppy, you and the puppy will soon be past the stage of "accidents" and ready to move on to a full and rewarding life together.

**ROLES OF DISCIPLINE, REWARD AND PUNISHMENT**
Discipline, training one to act in accordance with rules, brings order to life. It is as simple as that. Without discipline, particularly in a group society, chaos will reign supreme and the group will eventually perish. Humans and canines are social animals and need some form of discipline in order to function effectively. They must procure food, reproduce to keep their species going and protect their home base and their young.

If there were no discipline in the lives of social animals, they would eventually die from starvation and/or predation by other stronger animals. In the case of domestic canines, discipline in their lives is needed in order for them to understand how their pack (you and other family members) functions and how they must act in order to survive.

A large humane society in a highly populated area recently surveyed dog owners regarding their satisfaction with their relationships with their dogs. People who had trained their dogs were 75% more satisfied with their pets than those who had never trained their dogs.

Dr. Edward Thorndike, a renowned psychologist, established *Thorndike's Theory of Learning*, which states that a behavior that results in a pleasant event tends to be repeated. Furthermore, it concludes that a behavior that results in an unpleasant event tends not to be repeated. It is this theory upon which training methods are based today. For example, if you manipulate a dog to perform a specific behavior and reward him for doing it, he is likely to do it again because he enjoyed the end result.

Occasionally, punishment, a penalty inflicted for an offense, is necessary. The best type of punishment often comes from an outside source. For example, a child is told not to touch the stove because he may get burned. He disobeys and touches the

**TRAINING RULES**
If you want to be successful in training your dog, you have four rules to obey yourself:
1. Develop an understanding of how a dog thinks.
2. Do not blame the dog for lack of communication.
3. Define your dog's personality and act accordingly.
4. Have patience and be consistent.

stove. In doing so, he receives a burn. From that time on, he respects the heat of the stove and avoids contact with it. Therefore, a behavior that results in an unpleasant event tends not to be repeated.

A good example of a dog's learning the hard way is the dog who chases the house cat. He is told many times to leave the cat alone, yet he persists in teasing the cat. Then, one day, the dog begins chasing the cat but the cat turns and swipes a claw across the dog's face, leaving the dog with a painful gash on his nose. The final result is that the dog stops chasing the cat.

## HONOR AND OBEY

Dogs are the most honorable animals in existence. They consider another species (humans) as their own. They interface with you. You are their leader. Puppies perceive children to be on their level; their actions around small children are different from their behavior around their adult masters.

## TRAINING EQUIPMENT

### COLLAR AND LEASH

For an Irish Terrier, the collar and leash that you use for training must be one with which you are easily able to work, not too heavy for the dog and perfectly safe.

Much of your pup's behavior, good and bad, stems from what you do to mold it. For example, making sure that your pup has safe toys to keep him occupied will prevent him from getting into dangerous situations or resorting to destructive behaviors.

### TREATS

Have a bag of treats on hand; something nutritious and easy to swallow works best. Use a soft treat, a chunk of cheese or a piece of cooked chicken rather than a dry biscuit. By the time the dog has finished chewing a dry treat, he will forget why he is being rewarded in the first place!

Using food rewards will not teach a dog to beg at the table—the only way to teach a dog to beg at the table is to give him food from the table. In training, rewarding the dog with a food treat will help him associate praise and the treats with learning new behaviors that obviously please his owner.

### TRAINING BEGINS: ASK THE DOG A QUESTION

In order to teach your dog anything, you must first get his attention. After all, he cannot learn anything if he is looking away from you with his mind on something else.

To get your dog's attention, ask him "School?" and immediately walk over to him and give him a treat as you tell him "Good dog." Wait a minute or two and repeat the routine, this time with a treat in your hand as you approach within a foot of the dog. Do not go directly to him, but stop about a foot short of him and hold out the treat as you ask "School?" He will see you approaching with a treat in your hand and most likely begin walking toward you. As you meet, give him the treat and praise again.

The third time, ask the question, have a treat in your hand and walk only a short distance toward the dog so that he must walk almost all the way to you. As he reaches you, give him the treat and praise again.

By this time, the dog will probably be getting the idea that if he pays attention to you, especially when you ask that question, it will pay off in treats and enjoyable activities for him. In other words, he learns that "school" means doing great things with you that are fun and that result in positive attention for him.

Remember that the dog does not understand your verbal language; he only recognizes sounds. Your question translates to a series of sounds for him, and those sounds become the signal to go to you and pay attention. The dog learns that if he does this, he will get to interact with you plus receive treats and praise.

## THE BASIC COMMANDS

### TEACHING SIT

Now that you have the dog's attention, attach his leash and hold it in your left hand, and hold a food treat in your right hand. Place your food hand at the dog's nose and let him lick the treat but not take it from you. Say "Sit" and slowly raise your food hand from in front of the dog's nose up over his head so that he is looking at the ceiling. As he bends his head upward, he will have to bend his knees to maintain his balance. As he bends his knees, he will assume a sit position. At that point, release the food treat and praise lavishly with comments such as "Good dog!

Good sit!" Remember to always praise enthusiastically, because dogs relish verbal praise from their owners and feel so proud of themselves whenever they accomplish a behavior.

You will not use food forever in getting the dog to obey your commands. Food is only used to teach new behaviors and, once the dog knows what you want when you give a specific command, you will wean him off the food treats but still maintain the verbal praise. After all, you will always have your voice with you, and there will be many times when you have no food rewards but expect the dog to obey.

To teach the sit exercise, you can guide your dog into the correct position for the first few times to show him what's expected.

### TEACHING DOWN

Teaching the down exercise is easy when you understand how the dog perceives the down position, and it is very difficult when you do not. Dogs perceive the down position as a submissive one; therefore, teaching the down exercise by using a forceful method can sometimes make the dog develop such a fear of the down that he either runs away when you say "Down" or he attempts to snap at the person who tries to force him down.

Have the dog sit close alongside your left leg, facing in the same direction as you are. Hold the leash in your left hand and a food treat in your right. Now place your left hand lightly on the top of the dog's shoulders where they meet above the spinal cord. Do not push down on the dog's shoulders; simply rest your left hand there so you can guide the dog to lie down close to your left leg rather than to swing away from your side when he drops.

Now place the food hand at the dog's nose, say "Down" very softly (almost a whisper) and slowly lower the food hand to the dog's front feet. When the food hand reaches the floor, begin moving it forward along the floor in front of the dog. Keep talking softly to the dog, saying things like "Do you want this treat? You can do this, good dog." Your reassuring tone of voice will help calm the dog as he tries to follow the food hand in order to get the treat.

When the dog's elbows touch the floor, release the food and praise softly. Try to get the dog to maintain that down position for several seconds before you let him sit up again. The goal here is to get the dog to settle down and not feel threatened in the down position.

### DOUBLE JEOPARDY

A dog in jeopardy never lies down. He stays alert on his feet because instinct tells him that he may have to run away or fight for his survival. Therefore, if a dog feels threatened or anxious, he will not lie down. Consequently, it is important to keep the dog calm and relaxed as he learns the down exercise.

## Teaching Stay

It is easy to teach the dog to stay in either a sit or a down position. Again, we use food and praise during the teaching process as we help the dog to understand exactly what it is that we are expecting him to do.

To teach the sit/stay, start with the dog sitting on your left side as before and hold the leash in your left hand. Have a food treat in your right hand and place your food hand at the dog's nose. Say "Stay" and step out on your right foot to stand directly in front of the dog, toe to toe, as he licks and nibbles the treat. Be sure to keep his head facing upward to maintain the sit position. Count to five and then swing around to stand next to the dog again with him on your left. As soon as you get back to the original position, release

the food and praise lavishly.

To teach the down/stay, do the down as previously described. As soon as the dog lies down, say "Stay" and step out on your right foot just as you did in the sit/stay. Count to five and then return to stand beside the dog with him on your left side. Release the treat and praise as always.

Within a week or ten days, you can begin to add a bit of distance between you and your dog when you leave him. When you do, use your left hand open with the palm facing the dog as a stay signal, much the same as the hand signal a police officer uses to stop traffic at an intersection. Hold the food treat in your right hand as before, but this time the food will not be touching the dog's nose. He will watch the food hand and quickly learn that he is going to get that treat as soon as you return to his side.

When you can stand 3 feet

*Once your Irish is comfortable in the down position, you can progress to the down/stay.*

## CONSISTENCY PAYS OFF

Dogs need consistency in their feeding schedule, exercise and relief visits, and in the verbal commands you use. If you use "Stay" on Monday and "Stay here, please" on Tuesday, you will confuse your dog. Don't demand perfect behavior during training sessions and then let him have the run of the house the rest of the day. Above all, lavish praise on your pet consistently every time he does something right. The more he feels he is pleasing you, the more willing he will be to learn.

You can enjoy the company of your Irish Terrier wherever you go, as long as his safety is kept in mind and you know that he will reliably respond to you when called.

seems, is never to teach the word "come."

At times when an owner most wants his dog to come when called, the owner is likely to be upset or anxious and he allows these feelings to come through in the tone of his voice when he calls his dog. Hearing that desperation in his owner's voice, the dog fears the results of going to him and therefore either disobeys outright or runs in the opposite direction. The secret, therefore, is to teach the dog a game and, when you want him to come to you, simply play the game. It is practically a no-fail solution!

To begin, have several members of your family take a few food treats and each go into a different room in the house. Everyone takes turns calling the dog, and each person should celebrate the dog's finding him with a treat and lots of happy praise. When a person calls the dog, he is actually inviting the dog to find him and to get a treat as a reward for "winning."

away from your dog for 30 seconds, you can then begin building time and distance in both stays. Eventually, the dog can be expected to remain in the stay position for prolonged periods of time until you return to him or call him to you. Always praise lavishly when he stays.

### TEACHING COME

If you make teaching "come" an exciting experience, you should never have a student who does not love the game or who fails to come when called. The secret, it

### COMMAND STANCE

Stand up straight and authoritatively when giving your dog commands. Do not issue commands when lying on the floor or lying on your back on the sofa. If you are on your hands and knees when you give a command, your dog will think you are positioning yourself to play.

### "COME" . . . BACK

Never call your dog to come to you for a correction or scold him when he reaches you. That is the quickest way to turn a come command into "Go away fast!" Dogs think only in the present tense, and your dog will connect the scolding with coming to you, not with the misbehavior of a few moments earlier.

A few turns of the "Where are you?" game and the dog will understand that everyone is playing the game and that each person has a big celebration awaiting the dog's success at locating him. Once the dog learns to love the game, simply calling out "Where are you?" will bring him running from wherever he is when he hears that all-important question.

The come command is recognized as one of the most important things to teach a dog, but there are trainers who work with thousands of dogs and never use the actual word "come." Yet these dogs will race to respond to a person who uses the dog's name followed by "Where are you?" For example, a woman has a 12-year-old companion dog who went blind, but who never fails to locate her owner when asked, "Where are you?"

Children, in particular, love to play this game with their dogs. Children can hide in smaller

places like a shower stall or bathtub, behind a bed or under a table. The dog needs to work a little bit harder to find these hiding places, but, when he does, he loves to celebrate with a treat and a tussle with a favorite youngster.

### TEACHING HEEL

Heeling means that the dog walks beside the owner without pulling. It takes time and patience on the

If yours is a show dog, you will need to teach the dog to stand and to stay for longer periods of time. A dog must wait politely in the ring for his turn with the judge.

### HOW TO WEAN THE "TREAT HOG"

If you have trained your dog by rewarding him with a treat each time he performs a command, he may soon decide that, without the treat, he won't sit, stay or come. The best way to fix this problem is to start asking your dog to do certain commands twice before being rewarded. Slowly increase the number of commands given and then vary the number: three sits and a treat one day, five sits for a biscuit the next day, etc. Your dog will soon realize that there is no set number of sits before he gets his reward and he'll likely do it the first time you ask in the hope of being rewarded sooner rather than later.

owner's part to succeed at teaching the dog that he (the owner) will not proceed unless the dog is walking calmly beside him. Neither pulling out ahead on the leash nor lagging behind is acceptable.

Begin by holding the leash in your left hand as the dog sits beside your left leg. Move the loop end of the leash to your right hand, but keep your left hand short on the leash so that it keeps the dog in close next to you.

Say "Heel" and step forward on your left foot. Keep the dog close to you and take three steps. Stop and have the dog sit next to you in what we now call the heel position. Praise verbally, but do not touch the dog. Hesitate a moment and begin again with "Heel," taking three steps and stopping, at which point the dog is told to sit again.

Your goal here is to have the dog walk those three steps without pulling on the leash. Once he will walk calmly beside you for three steps without pulling, increase the number of steps you take to five. When he will walk politely beside you while you take five steps, you can increase the length of your walk to ten steps. Keep increasing the length of your stroll until the dog will walk quietly beside you without pulling as long as you want him to heel. When you stop heeling, indicate to the dog that the exercise is over by verbally praising as you pet him and say "OK, good dog." The "OK" is used as a release word, meaning that the exercise is finished and the dog is free to relax.

If you are dealing with a dog who insists on pulling you around, simply "put on your brakes" and stand your ground until the dog realizes that the two of you are not going anywhere until he is beside you and moving at your pace, not his. It may take some time just standing there to convince the dog that you are the leader and that you will be the one to decide on the direction and speed of your travel.

## TUG OF WALK?
If you begin teaching the heel by taking long walks and letting the dog pull you along, he misinterprets this action as an acceptable form of taking a walk. When you pull back on the leash to counteract his pulling, he reads that tug as a signal to pull even harder!

Each time the dog looks up at you or slows down to give a slack leash between the two of you, quietly praise him and say, "Good heel. Good dog." Eventually, the dog will begin to respond and within a few days he will be walking politely beside you without pulling on the leash. At first, the training sessions should be kept short and very positive; soon the dog will be able to walk nicely with you for increasingly longer distances. Remember also to give the dog free time and the opportunity to run and play when you have finished heel practice.

### WEANING OFF FOOD IN TRAINING
Food is used in training new behaviors. Once the dog understands what behavior goes with a specific command, it is time to start weaning him off the food treats. At first, give a treat after each exercise. Then, start to give a treat only after every other exercise. Mix up the times when you offer a food reward and the times when you only offer praise so that the dog will never know when he is going to receive both food and praise and when he is going to receive only praise. This is called a variable ratio reward system. It proves successful because there is always the chance that the owner will produce a treat, so the dog never stops trying for that reward. No matter what, *always* give verbal praise.

### OBEDIENCE CLASSES
It is a good idea to enroll in an obedience class if one is available in your area. If yours is a show dog, classes to prepare you and

Begin teaching the heel in a fenced-in area, and then see how your Irish does on walks around the neighborhood, where there will be more distractions.

**Heeling means that you are the one who sets the pace, and the dog must adjust his gait to match yours.**

own innovative ways, but his desire to please you will eventually win out. It helps if you keep your sense of humor! The major problem to overcome is the Irish Terrier's intolerance of other dogs. Once that is accomplished, the Irish is a competitive participant, thoroughly enjoyable to work with.

## OTHER ACTIVITIES FOR LIFE

Whether a dog is trained in the structured environment of a class or alone with his owner at home, there are many activities that can bring fun and rewards to both owner and dog once they have mastered basic control.

Teaching the dog to help out around the home, in the garden or on the farm provides great satisfaction to both dog and owner. In

your Irish for the show ring would be more appropriate. Many areas have dog clubs that offer basic obedience training as well as preparatory classes for obedience competition. There are also local dog trainers who offer similar classes.

At obedience trials, dogs can earn titles at various levels of competition. The beginning levels of obedience competition include basic behaviors such as sit, down, heel, etc. The more advanced levels of competition include jumping, retrieving, scent discrimination and signal work. The advanced levels require a dog and owner to put a lot of time and effort into their training. The titles that can be earned at these levels of competition are very prestigious.

The few Irish that compete in obedience do quite well. Training for obedience may be difficult in the beginning due to the dog's

### LANGUAGE BARRIER

Dogs do not understand our language and have to rely on tone of voice more than just words or sound. They can be trained to react to a certain sound, at a certain volume. If you say "No, Oliver" in a very soft, pleasant voice, it will not have the same meaning as "No, Oliver!!" when you raise your voice. You should never use the dog's name during a reprimand, just the command "No!" You never want the dog to associate his name with a negative experience or reprimand.

**THE STUDENT'S STRESS TEST**

During training sessions, you must be able to recognize signs of stress in your dog such as:

• tucking his tail between his legs
• lowering his head
• shivering or trembling
• standing completely still or running away
• panting and/or salivating
• avoiding eye contact
• flattening his ears back
• urinating submissively
• rolling over and lifting a leg
• grinning or baring teeth
• aggression when restrained

If your four-legged student displays these signs, he may just be nervous or intimidated. The training session may have been too lengthy, with not enough praise and affirmation. Stop for the day and try again tomorrow.

is good for man and dog alike, and the bond that they develop together is priceless. The rule for backpacking with any dog is never to expect the dog to carry more than one-sixth of his body weight.

If you are interested in participating in organized competition with your Irish Terrier, there are activities other than obedience in which you and your dog can become involved. Every terrier delights in going to ground, and many breed clubs offer earthdog tests for terriers, which test the dog's instinctive abilities. In addition, there are various types of all-breed events, such as tracking, which is open to all breeds with a nose!

Agility is a popular sport in which dogs run through obstacle courses that include various jumps, tunnels and other exercises to test the dog's speed and coordination. The owners run beside their dogs to give commands and to guide them through the course. Training for agility can begin once the dog is 12 months of age. Agility should only be undertaken when the owner is in complete control of his Irish, or there could be confrontations with perceived adversaries (i.e., any other dog in the class). Although competitive, the focus in agility is on fun—it's fun to do, fun to watch and great exercise.

addition, the dog's help makes life a little easier for his owner and raises his stature as a valued companion to his family. It helps give the dog a purpose by occupying his mind and providing an outlet for his energy.

Backpacking is an exciting and healthy activity that the dog can be taught without assistance from more than his owner. The exercise of walking and climbing

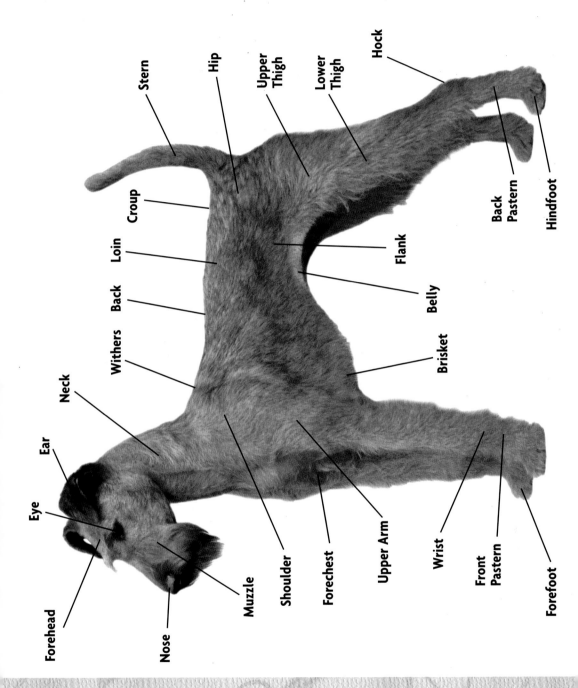

# PHYSICAL STRUCTURE OF THE IRISH TERRIER

# HEALTH CARE OF YOUR

# IRISH TERRIER

Dogs suffer from many of the same physical illnesses as people and might even share many of the same psychological problems. Since people usually know more about human diseases than canine maladies, many of the terms used in this chapter will be familiar but not necessarily those used by vets. For example, we will use the familiar term *x-ray* instead of *radiograph*. We will also use the familiar term *symptoms*, even though dogs don't have symptoms, which are verbal descriptions of something the patient feels or observes himself that he regards as abnormal. Dogs have *clinical signs* since they cannot speak, so we have to look for these clinical signs...but we still use the term *symptoms* in this book.

Medicine is a constantly changing art, with of course scientific input as well. Things alter as we learn more and more about basic sciences such as genetics and biochemistry, and have use of more sophisticated imaging techniques like Computer Aided Tomography (CAT scans) or Magnetic Resonance Imaging (MRI scans). There is academic dispute about many canine maladies, so different vets treat them in different ways. For example, some vets place a greater emphasis on surgical treatments than others.

## SELECTING A QUALIFIED VET

Your selection of a vet should be based on personal recommendation for his skills with small animals, especially dogs, and, if possible, terriers. If the vet is based nearby, it will be helpful because you might have an emergency or need to make multiple visits for treatments.

All vets are licensed and capable of dealing with routine medical issues such as infections, injuries and the promotion of health (for example, by vaccination). If the problem affecting your dog is more complex, your vet will refer your pet to someone with a more detailed knowledge of what is wrong. This will usually be a specialist at the nearest university veterinary school who concentrates in veterinary dermatology, veterinary ophthalmology, etc.; whatever field is relevant to your dog's problem.

Veterinary procedures are very

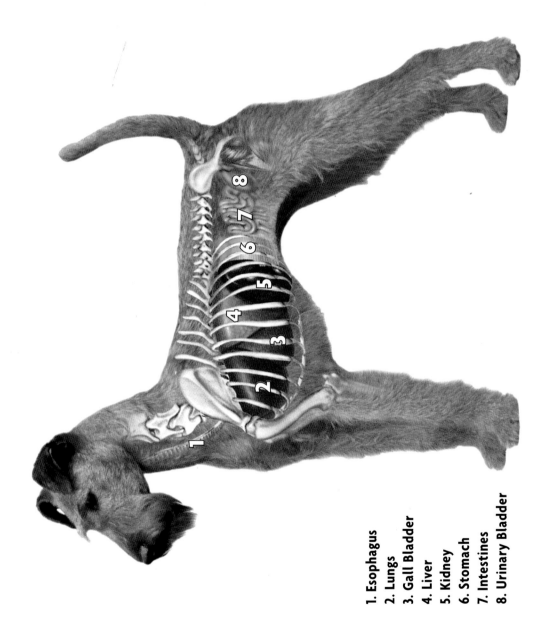

1. Esophagus
2. Lungs
3. Gall Bladder
4. Liver
5. Kidney
6. Stomach
7. Intestines
8. Urinary Bladder

INTERNAL ORGANS OF THE IRISH TERRIER

costly and, as the treatments available improve, they are going to become more expensive. It is quite acceptable to discuss matters of cost with your vet; if there is more than one treatment option, cost may be a factor in deciding which route to take. It is also acceptable to compare costs among vets or to get a second opinion, although it is courteous to advise the vets concerned.

Insurance against veterinary cost is also becoming very popular. Some policies cover emergencies such as surgery after a car accident, while others are more extensive and may offer coverage for routine veterinary procedures.

## PREVENTATIVE MEDICINE

It is much easier, less costly and more effective to practice preventative medicine than to fight bouts of illness and disease. Properly bred puppies of all breeds come from parents that were selected based upon their genetic-disease profiles. The puppies' mother should have been vaccinated, free of all internal and external parasites and properly nourished. For these reasons, a visit to the vet who cared for the dam is recommended if at all possible. The dam passes disease resistance to her puppies, which should last from eight to ten weeks. Unfortunately, she can also pass on parasites and infection. This is why knowledge about her health is useful in learn-

**Breakdown of Veterinary Income by Category**

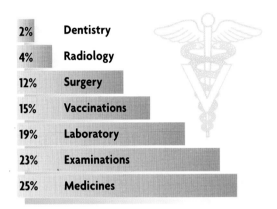

| | |
|---|---|
| 2% | Dentistry |
| 4% | Radiology |
| 12% | Surgery |
| 15% | Vaccinations |
| 19% | Laboratory |
| 23% | Examinations |
| 25% | Medicines |

A typical vet's income, categorized according to services performed. This survey dealt with small-animal (pets) practices.

ing more about the health of the puppies.

### WEANING TO FIVE MONTHS OLD

Puppies should be weaned by the time they are two months old. An Irish puppy that remains for at least ten weeks with his mother and littermates usually adapts better to other dogs and people later in his life.

Sometimes new owners have their puppy examined by a vet immediately, which is a good idea unless the puppy is overtired by a long journey. In that case, an appointment for the pup should be arranged for the next day after bringing him home.

At the first visit to the vet, the puppy will have his teeth examined and have his skeletal conformation and general health checked prior to certification by the vet. Puppies in certain breeds have

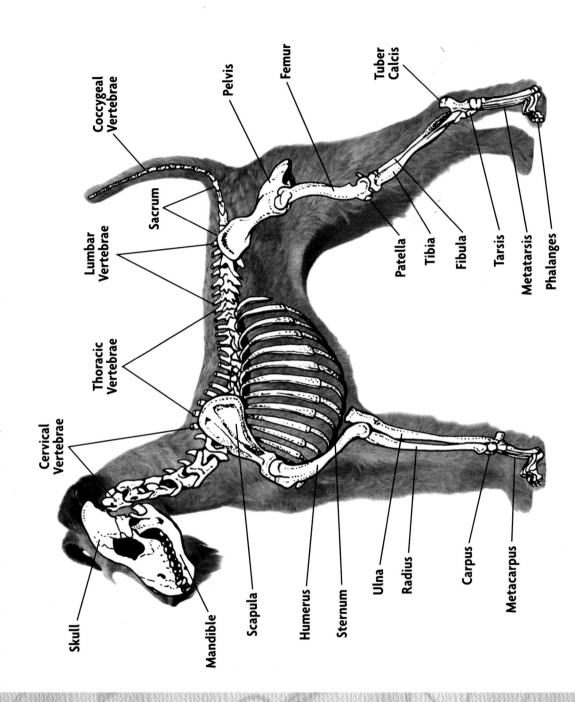

Coccygeal Vertebrae

Pelvis

Femur

Tuber Calcis

Sacrum

Lumbar Vertebrae

Patella

Tibia

Fibula

Tarsis

Metatarsis

Phalanges

Thoracic Vertebrae

Cervical Vertebrae

Skull

Mandible

Scapula

Humerus

Sternum

Ulna

Radius

Carpus

Metacarpus

# SKELETAL STRUCTURE OF THE IRISH TERRIER

problems with their kneecaps, cataracts and other eye problems, heart murmurs and undescended testicles. They may also have personality problems and your vet might have training in temperament evaluation. At this time, the vet also will set up a schedule to continue with the pup's vaccination program.

### VACCINATIONS

Most vaccinations are given by injection and should only be given by your vet. Both he and you should keep a record of the date of the injection, the identification of the vaccine and the amount given. Some vets give a first vaccination at eight weeks, but most dog breeders prefer the course not to commence until about ten weeks because of the risk of interaction with the antibodies produced by the mother. The vaccination schedule is usually based on a 15-day cycle. You must take your vet's advice as to when to vaccinate, as this may differ according to the vaccine used.

The usual vaccines contain immunizing doses of several different viruses such as distemper, parvovirus, parainfluenza and hepatitis. There are other vaccines available when the puppy is at risk. You should rely upon professional advice. This is

# HEALTH AND VACCINATION SCHEDULE

| AGE IN WEEKS: | 6TH | 8TH | 10TH | 12TH | 14TH | 16TH | 20-24TH | 52ND |
|---|---|---|---|---|---|---|---|---|
| Worm Control | ✔ | ✔ | ✔ | ✔ | ✔ | ✔ | ✔ | |
| Neutering | | | | | | | | ✔ |
| Heartworm | | ✔ | | ✔ | | ✔ | ✔ | |
| Parvovirus | ✔ | | ✔ | | ✔ | | ✔ | ✔ |
| Distemper | | ✔ | | ✔ | | ✔ | | ✔ |
| Hepatitis | | ✔ | | ✔ | | ✔ | | ✔ |
| Leptospirosis | | | | | | | | ✔ |
| Parainfluenza | ✔ | | ✔ | | ✔ | | | ✔ |
| Dental Examination | | ✔ | | | | | ✔ | ✔ |
| Complete Physical | | ✔ | | | | | ✔ | ✔ |
| Coronavirus | | | | ✔ | | | ✔ | ✔ |
| Canine Cough | ✔ | | | | | | | |
| Hip Dysplasia | | | | | | | | ✔ |
| Rabies | | | | | | | ✔ | |

Vaccinations are not instantly effective. It takes about two weeks for the dog's immune system to develop antibodies. Most vaccinations require annual booster shots. Your vet should guide you in this regard.

# DISEASE REFERENCE CHART

| | What is it? | What causes it? | Symptoms |
|---|---|---|---|
| **Leptospirosis** | Severe disease that affects the internal organs; can be spread to people. | A bacterium, which is often carried by rodents, that enters through mucous membranes and spreads quickly throughout the body. | Range from fever, vomiting and loss of appetite in less severe cases to shock, irreversible kidney damage and possibly death in most severe cases. |
| **Rabies** | Potentially deadly virus that infects warm-blooded mammals. | Bite from a carrier of the virus, mainly wild animals. | 1st stage: dog exhibits change in behavior, fear. 2nd stage: dog's behavior becomes more aggressive. 3rd stage: loss of coordination, trouble with bodily functions. |
| **Parvovirus** | Highly contagious virus, potentially deadly. | Ingestion of the virus, which is usually spread through the feces of infected dogs. | Most common: severe diarrhea. Also vomiting, fatigue, lack of appetite. |
| **Canine cough** | Contagious respiratory infection. | Combination of types of bacteria and virus. Most common: *Bordetella bronchiseptica* bacteria and parainfluenza virus. | Chronic cough. |
| **Distemper** | Disease primarily affecting respiratory and nervous system. | Virus that is related to the human measles virus. | Mild symptoms such as fever, lack of appetite and mucus secretion progress to evidence of brain damage, "hard pad." |
| **Hepatitis** | Virus primarily affecting the liver. | Canine adenovirus type I (CAV-1). Enters system when dog breathes in particles. | Lesser symptoms include listlessness, diarrhea, vomiting. More severe symptoms include "blue-eye" (clumps of virus in eye). |
| **Coronavirus** | Virus resulting in digestive problems. | Virus is spread through infected dog's feces. | Stomach upset evidenced by lack of appetite, vomiting, diarrhea. |

especially true for the booster immunizations. Most vaccination programs require a booster when the puppy is a year old and once a year thereafter. In some cases, circumstances may require more or less frequent immunizations.

Canine cough, more formally known as tracheobronchitis, is immunized against with a vaccine that is sprayed into the dog's nostrils. Canine cough is usually included in routine vaccination, but it is often not as effective as the vaccines for other major diseases.

**FIVE MONTHS TO ONE YEAR OF AGE**
Unless you intend to breed or show your dog, neutering the puppy around six months of age is recommended. Most professionals recommend this, and responsible breeders will include a neuter/spay provision in sales agreements for pet-quality puppies.

Neutering/spaying has proven to be extremely beneficial to male and female dogs, respectively. Besides eliminating the possibility of pregnancy, it inhibits (but does not prevent) breast cancer in bitches and prostate cancer in male dogs. Opinions differ on the best age at which to neuter/spay, so discuss this with your vet.

Your vet should provide your puppy with a thorough dental evaluation at six months of age, ascertaining whether all of the permanent teeth have erupted properly. A home dental-care regimen should be initiated at six months, including brushing weekly and providing good dental devices (such as hard plastic or nylon bones). Regular dental care promotes healthy teeth, fresh breath and a longer life.

### DOGS OLDER THAN ONE YEAR

Continue to visit the vet at least once a year. There is no such disease as "old age," but bodily functions do change with age. The eyes and ears are no longer as efficient. Liver, kidney and intestinal functions often decline. Proper dietary changes, recommended by your vet, can make life more pleasant for your aging Irish Terrier and you.

### SKIN PROBLEMS

Vets are consulted by dog owners for skin problems more than for any other group of diseases or maladies. A dog's skin is as sensitive, if not more so, than human skin, and both suffer from almost the same ailments (though the occurrence of acne in most breeds is rare). For this reason, veterinary dermatology has developed into a specialty practiced by many vets.

Since many skin problems have visual symptoms that are almost identical, it requires the skill of an experienced veterinary dermatologist to identify and cure many of the more severe skin disorders. Pet shops sell many treatments for skin problems, but most of the treatments are directed at symptoms and not at the underlying problem(s). If your dog is suffering from a skin disorder, you should seek professional assistance as quickly as possible. As with all diseases, the earlier a problem is identified and treated, the more likely it is that the cure will be successful.

### HEREDITARY SKIN DISORDERS

Veterinary dermatologists are currently researching a number of skin disorders that are believed to have a hereditary basis. These inherited diseases are transmitted by both parents, who appear (phenotypically) normal but have a recessive gene for the disease, meaning that they carry, but are not affected by, the disease. These diseases pose serious problems to breeders because in some instances there are no methods of identifying carriers. Often the secondary diseases associated with these skin conditions are even more debilitating than the skin disorders themselves, including cancers and respiratory problems.

Your Irish Terrier loves the great outdoors, so be diligent in checking his skin and coat when he comes inside. Flowers, grasses and the like can be home to insects, allergens and other irritants that can cause your dog problems.

Among the hereditary skin disorders for which the mode of inheritance is known are acrodermatitis, cutaneous asthenia (Ehlers-Danlos syndrome), sebaceous adenitis, cyclic hematopoiesis, dermatomyositis, IgA deficiency, color dilution alopecia and nodular dermatofibrosis. Some of these disorders are limited to one or two breeds, while others affect a large number of breeds. All inherited diseases must be diagnosed and treated by a veterinary specialist.

### PARASITE BITES
Many of us are allergic to insect bites. The bites itch, erupt and may even become infected. Dogs have the same reaction to fleas, ticks and/or mites. When an insect lands on you, you have the chance to whisk it away with your hand. Unfortunately, when a dog is bitten by a flea, tick or mite, he can only scratch it away or bite it. By the time the dog has been bitten, the parasite has done some of its damage. It may also have laid eggs, which will cause further problems in the near future. The itching from parasite bites is probably due to the saliva injected into the site when the parasite sucks the dog's blood.

### AIRBORNE ALLERGIES
Just as humans suffer from hay fever during the pollinating season, many dogs suffer from the same allergies. When the pollen count is high, your dog might suffer, but don't expect him to sneeze and have a runny nose as a human would. Dogs react to pollen allergies in the same way they react to fleas—they scratch and bite themselves. Dogs, like humans, can be tested for allergens. Discuss the testing with your vet.

### AUTO-IMMUNE ILLNESSES
An auto-immune illness is one in which the immune system overacts and does not recognize parts of the affected person; rather, the immune system starts to react as if these parts were foreign and need to be destroyed. An example is rheumatoid arthritis, which occurs when the body does not recognize the joints, thus leading to a very painful and damaging reaction in the joints. This has nothing to do with age, so can occur in children or young dogs as well as adults. The wear-and-tear arthritis of the older person or dog is osteoarthritis.

Lupus is an auto-immune disease that affects dogs as well as people. It can take variable forms, affecting the kidneys, bones and skin. It can be fatal, so is treated with steroids, which can themselves have very significant side effects. The steroids calm down the allergic reaction to the body's tissues, which helps the lupus, but steroids also decrease the body's reaction to real foreign substances such as bacteria, and they also thin the skin and bones.

## FOOD PROBLEMS

### FOOD ALLERGIES

Some dogs can be allergic to many foods that are best-sellers and highly recommended by breeders and vets. Changing the brand of food that you buy may not eliminate the problem if the element to which the dog is allergic is contained in the new brand.

Recognizing a food allergy in a dog can be difficult. Humans often have rashes when they eat foods to which they are allergic, or have swelling of the lips or eyes. Dogs do not usually develop rashes, but react in the same way as they to an airborne or bite allergy—they itch, scratch and bite. While pollen allergies are usually seasonal, food allergies are year-round problems.

Diagnosis of food allergy is based on a two- to four-week dietary trial with a home-cooked diet fed to the exclusion of all other foods. The diet should consist of boiled rice or potato with a source of protein that the dog has never eaten before, such as fresh or frozen fish, lamb or even something as exotic as pheasant or ostrich (if this is not too expensive in your part of the country). Water has to be the only drink, and it is really important that no other foods are fed during this trial.

If the dog's condition improves, you will need to try the original diet once again to see if the itching resumes. If it does, then this confirms the diagnosis that the dog is allergic to his original diet. The treatment is long-term feeding of something that does not distress the dog's skin, which may be in the form of one of the commercially available hypoallergenic diets or the home-made diet that you created for the allergy trial.

### FOOD INTOLERANCE

Food intolerance is the inability of the dog to completely digest certain foods. This occurs because the dog does not have the chemicals necessary to digest some foodstuffs. These chemicals are called enzymes. All puppies have the enzymes necessary to digest canine milk, but some dogs do not have the enzymes to digest a very different form of milk that is commonly found in human households—milk from cows. In such dogs, drinking cows' milk results in loose bowels, stomach pains and the passage of gas.

Dogs often do not have the enzymes to digest soy or other beans. The treatment is to exclude the foodstuffs that upset your Irish Terrier's digestion.

# First Aid at a Glance

### Burns
Place the affected area under cool water; use ice if only a small area is burnt.

### Insect bites
Apply ice to relieve swelling; antihistamine dosed properly.

### Animal bites
Clean any bleeding area; apply pressure until bleeding subsides; go to the vet.

### Spider bites
Use cold compress and a pressurized pack to inhibit venom's spreading.

### Antifreeze poisoning
Induce vomiting with hydrogen peroxide. Seek *immediate* veterinary help!

### Fish hooks
Removal best handled by vet; hook must be cut in order to remove.

### Snake bites
Pack ice around bite; contact vet quickly; identify snake for proper antivenin.

### Car accident
Move dog from roadway with blanket; seek veterinary aid.

### Shock
Calm the dog; keep him warm; seek immediate veterinary help.

### Nosebleed
Apply cold compress to the nose; apply pressure to any visible abrasion.

### Bleeding
Apply pressure above the area; treat wound by applying a cotton pack.

### Heat stroke
Submerge dog in cold bath; cool down with fresh air and water; go to the vet.

### Frostbite/Hypothermia
Warm the dog with a warm bath, electric blankets or hot water bottles.

### Abrasions
Clean the wound and wash out thoroughly with fresh water; apply antiseptic.

 *Remember: an injured dog may attempt to bite a helping hand from fear and confusion. Always muzzle the dog before trying to offer assistance.*

A male dog flea,
*Ctenocephalides
canis.*

PHOTO BY JEAN CLAUDE REVY/PHOTOTAKE

### EXTERNAL PARASITES

#### FLEAS

Of all the problems to which dogs are prone, none is more well known and frustrating than fleas. Flea infestation is relatively simple to cure but difficult to prevent. Parasites that are harbored inside the body are a bit more difficult to eradicate but they are easier to control.

To control flea infestation, you have to understand the flea's life cycle. Fleas are often thought of as a summertime problem, but centrally heated homes have changed the patterns and fleas can be found at any time of the year. The most effective method of flea control is a two-stage approach: one stage to kill the adult fleas, and the other to control the development of pre-adult fleas. Unfortunately, no single active ingredient is effective against all stages of the life cycle.

**FLEA KILLER CAUTION—
"POISON"**
Flea-killers are poisonous. You should not spray these toxic chemicals on areas of a dog's body that he licks, including his genitals and his face. Flea killers taken internally are a better answer, but check with your vet in case internal therapy is not advised for your dog.

## LIFE CYCLE STAGES

During its life, a flea will pass through four life stages: egg, larva, pupa or nymph and adult. The adult stage is the most visible and irritating stage of the flea life cycle, and this is why the majority of flea-control products concentrate on this stage. The fact is that adult fleas account for only 1% of the total flea population, and the other 99% exist in pre-adult stages, i.e., eggs, larvae and nymphs. The pre-adult stages are barely visible to the naked eye.

## THE LIFE CYCLE OF THE FLEA

Eggs are laid on the dog, usually in quantities of about 20 or 30, several times a day. The adult female flea must have a blood meal before each egg-laying session. When first laid, the eggs will cling to the dog's hair, as the eggs are still moist. However, they will quickly dry out and fall from the dog, especially if the dog moves around or scratches. Many eggs will fall off in the dog's favorite area or an area in which he spends a lot of time, such as his bed.

Once the eggs fall from the dog onto the carpet or furniture, they will hatch into larvae. This takes from one to ten days. Larvae are not particularly mobile and will usually travel only a few inches from where they hatch. However, they do have a tendency to move away from bright light and heavy

**EN GARDE:
CATCHING FLEAS OFF GUARD!**
Consider the following ways to arm yourself against fleas:
• Add a small amount of pennyroyal or eucalyptus oil to your dog's bath. These natural remedies repel fleas.
• Supplement your dog's food with fresh garlic (minced or grated) and a hearty amount of brewer's yeast, both of which ward off fleas.
• Use a flea comb on your dog daily. Submerge fleas in a cup of bleach to kill them quickly.
• Confine the dog to only a few rooms to limit the spread of fleas in the home.
• Vacuum daily...and get all of the crevices! Dispose of the bag every few days until the problem is under control.
• Wash your dog's bedding daily. Cover cushions where your dog sleeps with towels, and wash the towels often.

traffic—under furniture and behind doors are common places to find high quantities of flea larvae.

The flea larvae feed on dead organic matter, including adult flea feces, until they are ready to change into adult fleas. Fleas will usually remain as larvae for around seven days. After this period, the larvae will pupate into protective pupae. While inside the pupae, the larvae will undergo metamorphosis and change into adult fleas. This can take as little time as a few days, but the adult fleas can remain inside the pupae waiting to hatch for up to two years. The pupae are signaled to hatch by certain stimuli, such as physical pressure—the pupae's being stepped on, heat from an animal's lying on the pupae or increased carbon-dioxide levels and vibrations—indicating that a suitable host is available.

Once hatched, the adult flea must feed within a few days. Once the adult flea finds a host, it will not leave voluntarily. It only becomes dislodged by grooming or the host animal's scratching.

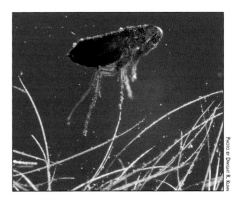

The adult flea will remain on the host for the duration of its life unless forcibly removed.

### TREATING THE ENVIRONMENT AND THE DOG

Treating fleas should be a two-pronged attack. First, the environment needs to be treated; this includes carpets and furniture, especially the dog's bedding and areas underneath furniture. The environment should be treated with a household spray containing an Insect Growth Regulator (IGR) and an insecticide to kill the adult fleas. Most IGRs are effective against eggs and larvae; they actually mimic the fleas' own hormones and stop the eggs and larvae from developing into adult fleas. There are currently no treatments available to attack the pupa stage of the life cycle, so the adult insecticide is used to kill the newly hatched adult fleas before they find a host. Most IGRs are active for many months, while

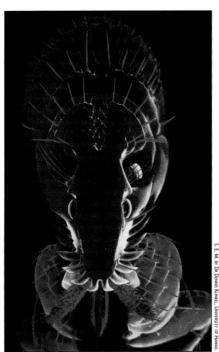

A scanning electron micrograph of a dog or cat flea, *Ctenocephalides*, magnified more than 100x. This image has been colorized for effect.

# THE LIFE CYCLE OF THE FLEA

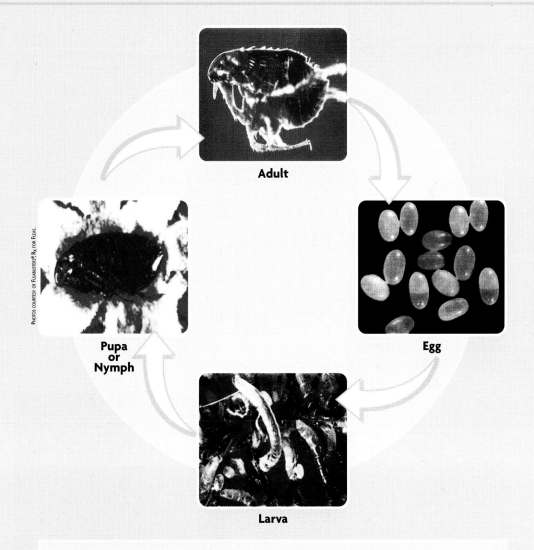

Adult

Egg

Larva

Pupa
or
Nymph

Fleas have been around for millions of years and have adapted to changing host animals. They are able to go through a complete life cycle in less than one month or they can extend their lives to almost two years by remaining as pupae or cocoons. They do not need blood or any other food for up to 20 months.

### INSECT GROWTH REGULATOR (IGR)

Two types of products should be used when treating fleas—a product to treat the pet and a product to treat the home. Adult fleas represent less than 1% of the flea population. The pre-adult fleas (eggs, larvae and pupae) represent more than 99% of the flea population and are found in the environment; it is in the case of pre-adult fleas that products containing an Insect Growth Regulator (IGR) should be used in the home.

IGRs are a new class of compounds used to prevent the development of insects. They do not kill the insect outright, but instead use the insect's biology against it to stop it from completing its growth. Products that contain methoprene are the world's first and leading IGRs. Used to control fleas and other insects, this type of IGR will stop flea larvae from developing and protect the house for up to seven months.

The American dog tick, *Dermacentor variabilis*, is probably the most common tick found on dogs. Look at the strength in its eight legs! No wonder it's hard to detach them.

adult insecticides are only active for a few days.

When treating with a household spray, it is a good idea to vacuum before applying the product. This stimulates as many pupae as possible to hatch into adult fleas. The vacuum cleaner should also be treated with an insecticide to prevent the eggs and larvae that have been collected in the vacuum bag from hatching.

The second stage of treatment is to apply an adult insecticide to the dog. Traditionally, this would be in the form of a collar or a spray, but more recent innovations include digestible insecticides that poison the fleas when they ingest the dog's blood. Alternatively, there are drops that, when placed on the back of the dog's neck, spread throughout the hair and skin to kill adult fleas.

### TICKS

Though not as common as fleas, ticks are found all over the tropical and temperate world. They don't bite, like fleas; they harpoon. They dig their sharp proboscis (nose) into the dog's skin and drink the blood. Their

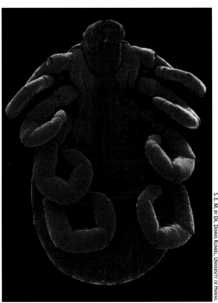

only food and drink is dog's blood. Dogs can get Lyme disease, Rocky Mountain spotted fever, tick bite paralysis and many other diseases from ticks. They may live where fleas are found and they like to hide in cracks or seams in walls. They are controlled the same way fleas are controlled.

The American dog tick, *Dermacentor variabilis*, may well be the most common dog tick in many geographical areas, especially those areas where the climate is hot and humid. Most dog ticks have life expectancies of a week to six months, depending upon climatic conditions. They can neither jump nor fly, but they can crawl slowly and can range up to 16 feet to reach a sleeping or unsuspecting dog.

## MITES

Just as fleas and ticks can be problematic for your dog, mites can also lead to an itchy nuisance. Microscopic in size, mites are related to ticks and generally take up permanent residence on their host animal— in this case, your dog! The term *mange* refers to any infestation caused by one of the mighty mites, of which there are six varieties that concern dog owners.

*Demodex* mites cause a condition known as demodicosis

### DEER-TICK CROSSING

The great outdoors may be fun for your dog, but it also is a home to dangerous ticks. Deer ticks carry a bacterium known as *Borrelia burgdorferi* and are most active in the autumn and spring. When infections are caught early, penicillin and tetracycline are effective antibiotics, but if left untreated the bacteria may cause neurological, kidney and cardiac problems as well as long-term trouble with walking and painful joints.

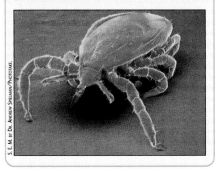

S.E.M. BY DR. ANDREW SPIELMAN/PHOTOTAKE.

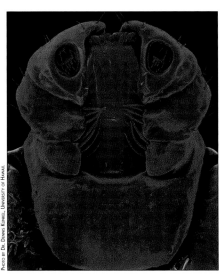

PHOTO BY DR. DENNIS KUNKEL, UNIVERSITY OF HAWAII.

The head of an American dog tick, *Dermacentor variabilis*, enlarged and colorized for effect.

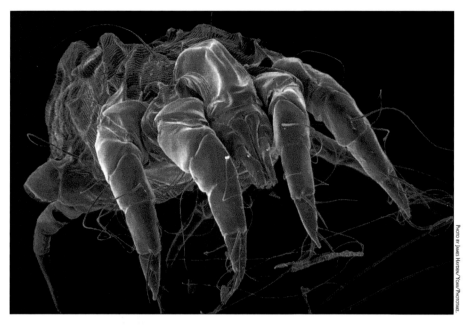

(sometimes called red mange or follicular mange), in which the mites live in the dog's hair follicles and sebaceous glands in larger-than-normal numbers. This type of mange is commonly passed from the dam to her puppies and usually shows up on the puppies' muzzles, though demodicosis is not transferable from one normal dog to another. Most dogs recover from this type of mange without any treatment, though topical therapies are commonly prescribed by the vet.

**Human lice look like dog lice; the two are closely related.**

The *Cheyletiellosis* mite is the hook-mouthed culprit associated with "walking dandruff," a condition that affects dogs as well as cats and rabbits. This mite lives on the surface of the animal's skin and is readily transferable through direct or indirect contact with an affected animal. The dandruff is present in the form of scaly skin, which may or may not be itchy. If not treated, this mange can affect a whole kennel of dogs and can be spread to humans as well.

The *Sarcoptes* mite causes intense itching on the dog in the form of a condition known as scabies or sarcoptic mange. The cycle of the *Sarcoptes* mite lasts about three weeks, and the mites live in the top layer of the dog's skin (epidermis), preferably in areas with little hair. Scabies is highly contagious and can be passed to humans. Sometimes an allergic reaction to the mite worsens the severe itching associated with sarcoptic mange.

Ear mites, *Otodectes cynotis,* lead to otodectic mange, which most commonly affects the outer ear canal of the dog, though other areas can be affected as well. Dogs with ear-mite infestation commonly scratch at their ears, causing further irritation, and shake their heads. Dark brown droppings in the outer ear confirm the diagnosis. Your vet can prescribe a treatment to flush out the ears and kill any eggs in the ears. A complete month of treatment is necessary to cure the mange.

Two other mites, less common in dogs, include *Dermanyssus gallinae* (the poultry or red mite) and *Eutrombicula alfreddugesi* (the North American mite associated with trombiculidiasis or chigger infestation). The poultry mite frequently lives on chickens, but can transfer to dogs who spend time near farm animals. Chigger infestation affects dogs in the

**NOT A DROP TO DRINK**
Never allow your dog to swim in polluted water or public areas where water quality can be suspect. Even perfectly clear water can harbor parasites, many of which can cause serious to fatal illnesses in canines. Areas inhabited by water-fowl and other wildlife are especially dangerous.

Central US who have exposure to woodlands. The types of mange caused by both of these mites are treatable by vets.

**INTERNAL PARASITES**
Most animals—fishes, birds and mammals, including dogs and humans—have worms and other parasites that live inside their bodies. According to Dr. Herbert R. Axelrod, the fish pathologist, there are two kinds of parasites: dumb and smart. The smart parasites live in peaceful cooperation with their hosts (symbiosis), while the dumb parasites kill their hosts. Most worm infections are relatively easy to control. If they are not controlled, they weaken the host dog to the point that other medical problems occur, but they do not kill the host as dumb parasites would.

**DO NOT MIX**
Never mix parasite-control products without first consulting your vet. Some products can become toxic when combined with others and can cause fatal consequences.

A brown dog tick, *Rhipicephalus sanguineus,* is an uncommon but annoying tick found on dogs.
PHOTO BY CAROLINA BIOLOGICAL SUPPLY/PHOTOTAKE.

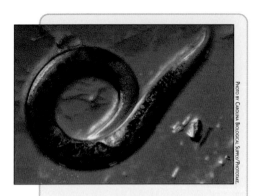

The roundworm *Rhabditis* can infect both dogs and humans.

The roundworm, *Ascaris lumbricoides.*

## ROUNDWORMS

Average-size dogs can pass 1,360,000 roundworm eggs every day. For example, if there were only 1 million dogs in the world, the world would be saturated with thousands of tons of dog feces. These feces would contain around 15,000,000,000 roundworm eggs.

Up to 31% of home yards and children's sand boxes in the US contain roundworm eggs.

Flushing dog's feces down the toilet is not a safe practice because the usual sewage treatments do not destroy roundworm eggs.

Infected puppies start shedding roundworm eggs at three weeks of age. They can be infected by their mother's milk.

## ROUNDWORMS

The roundworms that infect dogs are known scientifically as *Toxocara canis.* They live in the dog's intestines and shed eggs continually. It has been estimated that a dog produces about 6 or more ounces of feces every day. Each ounce of feces averages hundreds of thousands of roundworm eggs. There are no known areas in which dogs roam that do not contain roundworm eggs. The greatest danger of roundworms is that they infect people, too! It is wise to have your dog tested regularly for roundworms.

In young puppies, roundworms cause bloated bellies, diarrhea, coughing and vomiting, and are transmitted from the dam (through blood or milk). Affected puppies will not appear as animated as normal puppies. The worms appear spaghetti-like, measuring as long as 6 inches. Adult dogs can acquire roundworms through coprophagia (eating contaminated feces) or by killing rodents that carry roundworms.

Roundworm infection can kill puppies and cause severe problems in adults, as the hatched larvae travel to the lungs and trachea through the bloodstream. Cleanliness is the best preventative for roundworms. Always pick up after your dog and dispose of feces in appropriate receptacles.

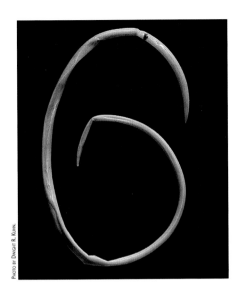

## HOOKWORMS

In the United States, dog owners have to be concerned about four different species of hookworm, the most common and most serious of which is *Ancylostoma caninum,* which prefers warm climates. The others are *Ancylostoma braziliense, Ancylostoma tubaeforme* and *Uncinaria stenocephala,* the latter of which is a concern to dogs living in the northern US and Canada, as this species prefers cold climates. Hookworms are dangerous to humans as well as to dogs and cats, and can be the cause of severe anemia due to iron deficiency. The worm uses its teeth to attach itself to the dog's intestines and changes the site of its attachment about six times per day. Each time the worm repositions itself, the dog loses blood and can become anemic. *Ancylostoma caninum* is the most likely of the four species to cause anemia in the dog.

Symptoms of hookworm infection include dark stools, weight loss, general weakness, pale coloration and anemia, as well as possible skin problems. Fortunately, hookworms are easily purged from the affected dog with a number of medications that have proven effective. Discuss these with your vet. Most heartworm preventatives include a hookworm insecticide as well.

Owners also must be aware that hookworms can infect humans, who can acquire the larvae through exposure to contaminated feces. Since the worms cannot complete their life cycle on a human, the worms simply infest the skin and cause irritation. This condition is known as cutaneous larva migrans syndrome. As a preventative, use disposable gloves or a "poop-scoop" to pick up your dog's droppings and prevent your dog (or neighborhood cats) from defecating in children's play areas.

The hookworm, *Ancylostoma caninum.*

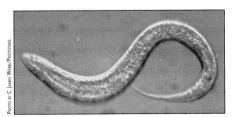

The infective stage of the hookworm larva.

## TAPEWORMS

Humans, rats, squirrels, foxes, coyotes, wolves and domestic dogs are all susceptible to tapeworm infection. Except in humans, tapeworms are usually not a fatal infection. Infected individuals can harbor 1000 parasitic worms.

Tapeworms, like some other types of worm, are hermaphroditic, meaning male and female in the same worm.

If dogs eat infected rats or mice, or anything else infected with tapeworm, they get the tapeworm disease. One month after attaching to a dog's intestine, the worm starts shedding eggs. These eggs are infective immediately. Infective eggs can live for a few months without a host animal.

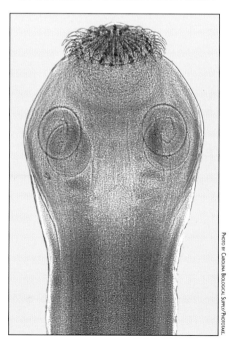

The head and rostellum (the round prominence on the scolex) of a tapeworm, which infects dogs and humans.

PHOTO BY CAROLINA BIOLOGICAL SUPPLY/PHOTOTAKE.

## TAPEWORMS

There are many species of tapeworm, all of which are carried by fleas! The most common tapeworm affecting dogs is known as *Dipylidium caninum*. The dog eats the flea and starts the tapeworm cycle. Humans can also be infected with tapeworms—so don't eat fleas! Fleas are so small that your dog could pass them onto your hands, your plate or your food and thus make it possible for you to ingest a flea that is carrying tapeworm eggs.

While tapeworm infection is not life-threatening in dogs (smart parasite!), it can be the cause of a very serious liver disease for humans. About 50% of the humans infected with *Echinococcus multilocularis*, a type of tapeworm that causes alveolar hydatid, perish.

## WHIPWORMS

In North America, whipworms are counted among the most common parasitic worms in dogs. The whipworm's scientific name is *Trichuris vulpis*. These worms attach themselves in the lower parts of the intestine, where they feed. Affected dogs may only experience upset tummies, colic and diarrhea. These worms, however, can live for months or years in the dog, beginning their larval stage in the small intestine, spending their adult stage in the large intestine and finally passing infective eggs through the dog's feet. The only way to detect whipworms is through a fecal examination, though this is not always foolproof. Treatment for whipworms is tricky, due to the worms' unusual life-cycle pattern, and very often dogs are reinfected due to exposure to infective eggs on the ground. The whipworm eggs can survive in the environment for as long as five years; thus, cleaning up droppings in your own backyard as well as in public places is absolutely essential for sanitation purposes and the health of your dog and others.

### THREADWORMS

Though less common than round-worms, hookworms and those previously mentioned, thread-worms concern dog owners in the Southwestern US and Gulf Coast area where the climate is hot and humid. Living in the small intes-tine of the dog, this worm measures a mere 2 millimeters and is round in shape. Like that of the whipworm, the threadworm's life cycle is very complex and the eggs and larvae are passed through the feces. A deadly disease in humans, *Strongyloides* readily infects people, and the handling of feces is the most common means of trans-mission. Threadworms are most often seen in young puppies; bloody diarrhea and pneumonia are symptoms. Sick puppies must be isolated and treated immedi-ately; vets recommend a follow-up treatment one month later.

## HEARTWORM PREVENTATIVES

There are many heartworm preventatives on the market, many of which are sold at your veterinarian's office. These products can be given daily or monthly, depending on the manufacturer's instructions. All of these preventatives contain chemical insecticides directed at killing heartworms, which leads to some controversy among dog owners. In effect, heartworm preventatives are neces-sary evils, though you should determine how necessary based on your pet's lifestyle. There is no doubt that heartworm is a dreadful disease that threatens the lives of dogs. However, the likelihood of your dog's being bitten by an infected mosquito is slim in most places, and a mosquito-repellent (or an herbal remedy such as Wormwood or Black Walnut) is much safer for your dog and will not compromise his immune system (the way heartworm preventatives will). Should you decide to use the tradi-tional preventative "medications," you can consider giving the pill every other or third month. Since the toxins in the pill will kill the heartworms at all stages of develop-ment, the pill would be effective in killing larvae, nymphs or adults and it takes four months for the larvae to reach the adult stage. Thus, there is no rationale to poison-ing the dog's system on a monthly basis. Lastly, do not give the pill during the winter months since there are no mosquitoes around to pass on their infection, unless you live in a tropical environment.

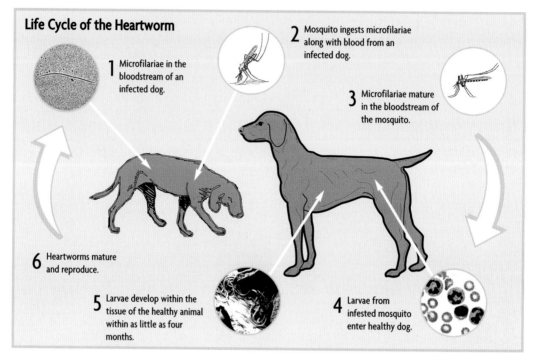

## Life Cycle of the Heartworm

1 Microfilariae in the bloodstream of an infected dog.

2 Mosquito ingests microfilariae along with blood from an infected dog.

3 Microfilariae mature in the bloodstream of the mosquito.

6 Heartworms mature and reproduce.

5 Larvae develop within the tissue of the healthy animal within as little as four months.

4 Larvae from infested mosquito enter healthy dog.

### HEARTWORMS

Heartworms are thin, extended worms up to 12 inches long, which live in a dog's heart and the major blood vessels surrounding it. Dogs may have up to 200 worms. Symptoms may be loss of energy, loss of appetite, coughing, development of a pot belly and anemia.

Heartworms are transmitted by mosquitoes. The mosquito drinks the blood of an infected dog and takes in larvae with the blood. The larvae, called microfilariae, develop within the body of the mosquito and are passed on to the next dog bitten after the larvae mature. It takes two to three weeks for the larvae to develop to the infective stage within the body of the mosquito. Dogs are usually treated at about six weeks of age and maintained on a prophylactic dose given monthly.

Blood testing for heartworms is not necessarily indicative of how seriously your dog is infected. Although this is a dangerous disease, it is not easy for a dog to be infected. Discuss the various preventatives with your vet, as there are many different types now available. Together you can decide on a safe course of prevention for your dog.

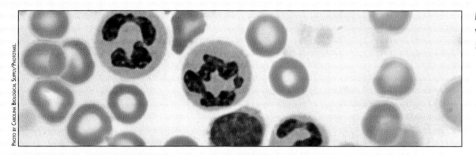

Photo by Carolina Biological Supply/Phototake.

Magnified heartworm larvae, *Dirofilaria immitis*.

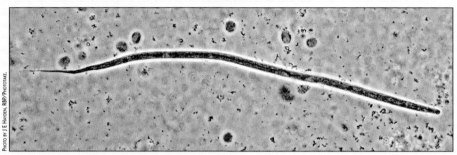

Photo by J. E. Hayden, RBP/Phototake.

Heartworm, *Dirofilaria immitis*.

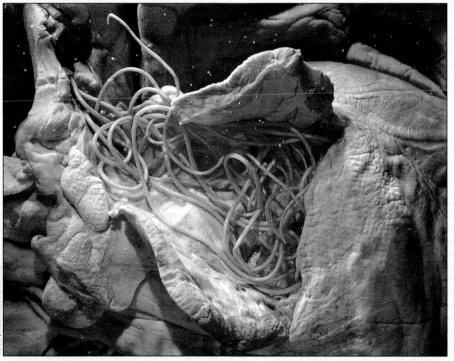

Photo by James E. Hayden, RFB/Phototake.

The heart of a dog infected with canine heartworm, *Dirofilaria immitis*.

# HOMEOPATHY:
## an alternative to conventional medicine

### "Less is Most"

Using this principle, the strength of a homeopathic remedy is measured by the number of serial dilutions that were undertaken to create it. The greater the number of serial dilutions, the greater the strength of the homeopathic remedy. The potency of a remedy that has been made by making a dilution of 1 part in 100 parts (or 1/100) is 1c or 1cH. If this remedy is subjected to a series of further dilutions, each one being 1/100, a more dilute and stronger remedy is produced. If the remedy is diluted in this way six times, it is called 6c or 6cH. A dilution of 6c is 1 part in 1,000,000,000,000. In general, higher potencies in more frequent doses are better for acute symptoms and lower potencies in more infrequent doses are more useful for chronic, long-standing problems.

## CURING OUR DOGS NATURALLY

Holistic medicine means treating the whole animal as a unique, perfect living being. Generally, holistic treatments do not suppress the symptoms that the body naturally produces, as do most medications prescribed by conventional doctors and vets. Holistic methods seek to cure disease by regaining balance and harmony in the patient's environment. Some of these methods include use of nutritional therapy, herbs, flower essences, aromatherapy, acupuncture, massage, chiropractic and, of course, the most popular holistic approach, homeopathy.

Homeopathy is a theory or system of treating illness with small doses of substances which, if administered in larger quantities, would produce the symptoms that the patient already has. This approach is often described as "like cures like." Although modern veterinary medicine is geared toward the "quick fix," homeopathy relies on the belief that, given the time, the body is able to heal itself and return to its natural, healthy state.

Choosing a remedy to cure a problem in our dogs is the difficult part of homeopathy. Consult with your vet for a professional diagnosis of your dog's symptoms. Often

these symptoms require immediate conventional care. If your vet is willing and knowledgeable, you may attempt a homeopathic remedy. Be aware that cortisone prevents homeopathic remedies from working. There are hundreds of possibilities and combinations to cure many problems in dogs, from basic physical problems such as excessive shedding, fleas or other parasites, unattractive doggy odor, bad breath, upset tummy, obesity, dry, oily or dull coat, diarrhea, ear problems or eye discharge (including tears and dry or mucousy matter), to behavioral abnormalities such as fear of loud noises, habitual licking, poor appetite, excessive barking and various phobias. From alumina to zincum metallicum, the remedies span the planet and the imagination…from flowers and weeds to chemicals, insect droppings, diesel smoke and volcanic ash.

# Using "Like to Treat Like"

Unlike conventional medicines that suppress symptoms, homeopathic remedies treat illnesses with small doses of substances that, if administered in larger quantities, would produce the symptoms that the patient already has. While the same homeopathic remedy can be used to treat different symptoms in different dogs, here are some interesting remedies and their uses.

### Apis Mellifica
(made from honey bee venom) can be used for allergies or to reduce swelling that occurs in acutely infected kidneys.

### Diesel Smoke
can be used to help control travel sickness.

### Calcarea Fluorica
(made from calcium fluoride, which helps harden bone structure) can be useful in treating hard lumps in tissues.

### Natrum Muriaticum
(made from common salt, sodium chloride) is useful in treating thin, thirsty dogs.

### Nitricum Acidum
(made from nitric acid) is used for symptoms you would expect to see from contact with acids, such as lesions, especially where the skin joins the linings of body orifices or openings such as the lips and nostrils.

### Symphytum
(made from the herb Knitbone, *Symphytum officianale*) is used to encourage bones to heal.

### Urtica Urens
(made from the common stinging nettle) is used in treating painful, irritating rashes.

# HOMEOPATHIC REMEDIES FOR YOUR DOG

| Symptom/Ailment | Possible Remedy |
|---|---|
| **ALLERGIES** | Apis Mellifica 30c, Astacus Fluviatilis 6c, Pulsatilla 30c, Urtica Urens 6c |
| **ALOPECIA** | Alumina 30c, Lycopodium 30c, Sepia 30c, Thallium 6c |
| **ANAL GLANDS** (BLOCKED) | Hepar Sulphuris Calcareum 30c, Sanicula 6c, Silicea 6c |
| **ARTHRITIS** | Rhus Toxicodendron 6c, Bryonia Alba 6c |
| **CATARACT** | Calcarea Carbonica 6c, Conium Maculatum 6c, Phosphorus 30c, Silicea 30c |
| **CONSTIPATION** | Alumina 6c, Carbo Vegetabilis 30c, Graphites 6c, Nitricum Acidum 30c, Silicea 6c |
| **COUGHING** | Aconitum Napellus 6c, Belladonna 30c, Hyoscyamus Niger 30c, Phosphorus 30c |
| **DIARRHEA** | Arsenicum Album 30c, Aconitum Napellus 6c, Chamomilla 30c, Mercurius Corrosivus 30c |
| **DRY EYE** | Zincum Metallicum 30c |
| **EAR PROBLEMS** | Aconitum Napellus 30c, Belladonna 30c, Hepar Sulphuris 30c, Tellurium 30c, Psorinum 200c |
| **EYE PROBLEMS** | Borax 6c, Aconitum Napellus 30c, Graphites 6c, Staphysagria 6c, Thuja Occidentalis 30c |
| **GLAUCOMA** | Aconitum Napellus 30c, Apis Mellifica 6c, Phosphorus 30c |
| **HEAT STROKE** | Belladonna 30c, Gelsemium Sempervirens 30c, Sulphur 30c |
| **HICCOUGHS** | Cinchona Deficinalis 6c |
| **HIP DYSPLASIA** | Colocynthis 6c, Rhus Toxicodendron 6c, Bryonia Alba 6c |
| **INCONTINENCE** | Argentum Nitricum 6c, Causticum 30c, Conium Maculatum 30c, Pulsatilla 30c, Sepia 30c |
| **INSECT BITES** | Apis Mellifica 30c, Cantharis 30c, Hypericum Perforatum 6c, Urtica Urens 30c |
| **ITCHING** | Alumina 30c, Arsenicum Album 30c, Carbo Vegetabilis 30c, Hypericum Perforatum 6c, Mezerium 6c, Sulphur 30c |
| **KENNEL COUGH** | Drosera 6c, Ipecacuanha 30c |
| **MASTITIS** | Apis Mellifica 30c, Belladonna 30c, Urtica Urens 1m |
| **MOTION SICKNESS** | Cocculus 6c, Petroleum 6c |
| **PATELLAR LUXATION** | Gelsemium Sempervirens 6c, Rhus Toxicodendron 6c |
| **PENIS PROBLEMS** | Aconitum Napellus 30c, Hepar Sulphuris Calcareum 30c, Pulsatilla 30c, Thuja Occidentalis 6c |
| **PUPPY TEETHING** | Calcarea Carbonica 6c, Chamomilla 6c, Phytolacca 6c |

## Recognizing a Sick Dog

Unlike colicky babies and cranky children, our canine charges cannot tell us when they are feeling ill. Therefore, there are a number of signs that owners can identify to know that their dogs are not feeling well.

**Take note for
physical manifestations such as:**

- unusual, bad odor, including bad breath
- excessive shedding
- wax in the ears, chronic ear irritation
- oily, flaky, dull haircoat
- mucus, tearing or similar discharge in the eyes
- fleas or mites
- mucus in stool, diarrhea
- sensitivity to petting or handling
- licking at paws, scratching face, etc.

**Keep an eye out for
behavioral changes as well including:**

- lethargy, idleness
- lack of patience or general irritability
- lack of appetite
- phobias (fear of people, loud noises, etc.)
- strange behavior, suspicion, fear
- coprophagia
- more frequent barking
- whimpering, crying

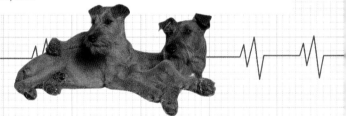

## Get Well Soon

You don't need a DVM to provide good TLC to your sick or recovering dog, but you do need to pay attention to some details that normally wouldn't bother him. The following tips will aid Fido's recovery and get him back on his paws again:

- Keep his space free of irritating smells, like heavy perfumes and air fresheners.
- Rest is the best medicine! Avoid harsh lighting that will prevent your dog from sleeping. Shade him from bright sunlight during the day and dim the lights in the evening.
- Keep the noise level down. Animals are more sensitive to sound when they are sick.

- Be attentive to any necessary temperature adjustments. A dog with a fever needs a cool room and cold liquids. A bitch that is whelping or recovering from surgery will be more comfortable in a warm room, consuming warm liquids and food.
- You wouldn't send a sick child back to school early, so don't rush your dog back into a full routine until he seems absolutely ready.

# Number-One Killer Disease in Dogs: CANCER

In every age, there is a word associated with a disease or plague that causes humans to shudder. In the 21st century, that word is "cancer." Just as cancer is the leading cause of death in humans, it claims nearly half the lives of dogs that die from a natural disease as well as half the dogs that die over the age of ten years.

Described as a genetic disease, cancer becomes a greater risk as the dog ages. Vets and dog owners have become increasingly aware of the threat of cancer to dogs. Statistics reveal that one dog in every five will develop cancer, the most common of which is skin cancer. Many cancers, including prostate, ovarian and breast cancer, can be avoided by spaying and neutering our dogs by the age of six months.

Early detection of cancer can save or extend a dog's life, so it is absolutely vital for owners to have their dogs examined by a qualified vet or oncologist immediately upon detection of any abnormality. Certain dietary guidelines have also proven to reduce the onset and spread of cancer. Foods based on fish rather than beef, due to the presence of Omega-3 fatty acids, are recommended. Other amino acids such as glutamine have significant benefits for canines, particularly those breeds that show a greater susceptibility to cancer.

Cancer management and treatments promise hope for future generations of canines. Since the disease is genetic, breeders should never breed a dog whose parents, grandparents and any related siblings have developed cancer. It is difficult to know whether to exclude an otherwise healthy dog from a breeding program as the disease does not manifest itself until the dog's senior years.

## RECOGNIZE CANCER WARNING SIGNS

Since early detection can possibly rescue your dog from becoming a cancer statistic, it is essential for owners to recognize the possible signs and seek the assistance of a qualified professional.

- Abnormal bumps or lumps that continue to grow
- Bleeding or discharge from any body cavity
- Persistent stiffness or lameness
- Recurrent sores or sores that do not heal
- Inappetence
- Breathing difficulties
- Weight loss
- Bad breath or odors
- General malaise and fatigue
- Eating and swallowing problems
- Difficulty urinating and defecating

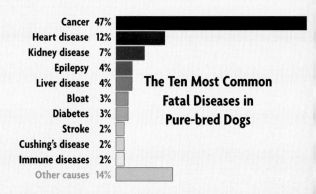

| Cancer | 47% |
| Heart disease | 12% |
| Kidney disease | 7% |
| Epilepsy | 4% |
| Liver disease | 4% |
| Bloat | 3% |
| Diabetes | 3% |
| Stroke | 2% |
| Cushing's disease | 2% |
| Immune diseases | 2% |
| Other causes | 14% |

**The Ten Most Common Fatal Diseases in Pure-bred Dogs**

# CDS: COGNITIVE DYSFUNCTION SYNDROME
## "OLD-DOG SYNDROME"

There are many ways to evaluate old-dog syndrome. Vets have defined CDS (cognitive dysfunction syndrome) as the gradual deterioration of cognitive abilities. These are indicated by changes in the dog's behavior. When a dog changes his routine response, and maladies have been eliminated as the cause of these behavioral changes, then CDS is the usual diagnosis.

More than half the dogs over eight years old suffer from some form of CDS. The older the dog, the more chance he has of suffering from CDS. In humans, doctors often dismiss the CDS behavioral changes as part of "winding down."

There are four major signs of CDS: frequent potty accidents inside the home, sleeping much more or much less than normal, acting confused and failing to respond to social stimuli.

## SYMPTOMS OF CDS

### FREQUENT POTTY ACCIDENTS
- *Urinates in the house.*
- *Defecates in the house.*
- *Doesn't signal that he wants to go out.*

### SLEEP PATTERNS
- *Moves much more slowly.*
- *Sleeps more than normal during the day.*
- *Sleeps less during the night.*

### CONFUSION
- *Goes outside and just stands there.*
- *Appears confused with a faraway look in his eyes.*
- *Hides more often.*
- *Doesn't recognize friends.*
- *Doesn't come when called.*
- *Walks around listlessly and without a destination.*

### FAILURE TO RESPOND TO SOCIAL STIMULI
- *Comes to people less frequently, whether called or not.*
- *Doesn't tolerate petting for more than a short time.*
- *Doesn't come to the door when you return home.*

# IRISH TERRIER

The term *old* is a qualitative term. For dogs, as well as for their masters, old is relative. Certainly we can all distinguish between a puppy Irish Terrier and an adult Irish Terrier—there are the obvious physical traits, such as size, appearance and facial expressions, as well as personality traits. Puppies and young dogs like to play with children. Children's natural exuberance is a good match for the seemingly endless energy of young dogs. They like to run, jump, chase and retrieve. When dogs grow older and cease their interaction with children, they are often thought of as being too old to keep pace with the children. On the other hand, if an Irish Terrier is only exposed to people with quieter lifestyles, his life will normally be less active and the decrease in his activity level as he ages will not be as obvious.

If people live to be 100 years old, dogs live to be 20 years old. While this might seem like a good rule of thumb, it is very inaccurate. When trying to compare dog years to human years, you cannot make a generalization about all

dogs. You can make the generalization that the average lifespan for an Irish Terrier is 12 to 14 years. Irish Terriers generally are considered physically mature at two to three years of age, but can reproduce even earlier. So, again to generalize, let's say that the first three years of a dog's life are like seven times that of comparable humans. That means a 3-year-old dog is like a 21-year-old human.

However, as the curve of comparison shows, there is no hard-and-fast rule for comparing dog and human ages. Small breeds tend to live longer than large breeds, some breeds' adolescent periods last longer than others' and some breeds experience rapid periods of growth. The comparison is made even more difficult, for, likewise, not all humans age at the same rate...and human females tend to live longer than human males.

## WHAT TO LOOK FOR IN SENIORS

Most vets and behaviorists use the seven-year mark as the time to consider a dog a senior. The term *senior* does not imply that the dog is geriatric and has begun to fail in mind and body. In fact, the Irish, being a terrier, may retain a puppyish energy for his entire life. Aging is essentially a slowing process. Humans readily admit that they feel a difference in their activity level from age 20 to 30, and then from 30 to 40, etc. By treating the seven-year-old dog as a senior, owners are able to implement certain therapeutic and preventative medical strategies with the help of their vets.

A special-care program for the senior dog should include at least two veterinary visits per year and screening sessions to determine the dog's health status, as well as nutritional counseling. Vets deter-mine the senior dog's health status through a blood smear for a complete blood count, serum chemistry profile with elec-trolytes, urinalysis, blood pressure check, electrocardiogram, ocular tonometry (pressure on the eyeball) and dental prophylaxis.

Such an extensive program for senior dogs is well advised before owners start to see the obvious physical signs of aging, such as slower and inhibited movement, graying, increased sleep/nap peri-ods and disinterest in play and other activity. This preventative program promises a longer, healthier life for the aging dog. Among the physical problems common in aging dogs are the loss

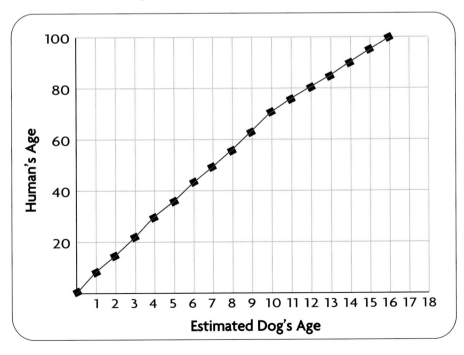

of sight and hearing, arthritis, kidney and liver failure, diabetes mellitus, heart disease and Cushing's disease (a hormonal disease).

In addition to the physical manifestations discussed, there are some behavioral changes and problems related to aging dogs. Dogs suffering from hearing or vision loss, dental discomfort or arthritis can become aggressive. Likewise, the near-deaf and/or blind dog may be startled more easily and react in an unexpectedly aggressive manner. Seniors suffering from senility can become more impatient and irritable. Housesoiling accidents are associated with loss of mobility, kidney problems and loss of sphincter control as well as plaque accumulation, physiological brain changes and reactions to medications. Older dogs, just like young puppies, suffer from separation anxiety, which can lead to excessive barking, whining, housesoiling and destructive behavior. Seniors may become fearful of everyday sounds, such as vacuum cleaners, heaters, thunder and passing traffic. Some dogs have difficulty sleeping, due to discomfort, the need for frequent potty visits and the like.

Owners should avoid spoiling the older dog with too many treats. Obesity is a common problem in older dogs and subtracts years from their lives. Keep the senior dog as trim as possible, since excessive weight puts additional stress on the body's vital organs. Some breeders recommend supplementing the diet with foods high in fiber and lower in calories. Adding fresh vegetables and marrow broth to the senior's diet makes a tasty, low-calorie, low-fat supplement. Vets also offer specialty diets for senior dogs that are worth exploring.

Your dog, as he nears his twilight years, needs your patience and good care more than ever. Never punish an older dog for an accident or abnormal behavior. For all the years of love, protection and companionship that your dog has provided, he deserves special attention and courtesies. The older dog may need to relieve himself at 3 a.m. because he can no longer "hold it" for eight hours. Older dogs may not be able to remain crated for more than two or three hours. It may be time to give up a sofa or chair to your old friend. Although

**AGING ADDITIVES**
A healthy diet is important for dogs of all ages, but older dogs may benefit from the addition of supplements like antioxidants, which fight the aging process, and vitamin B, which aids the kidneys. Check with your vet before adding these or any supplements to your pet's diet.

he may not seem as enthusiastic about your attention and petting, he does appreciate the considerations you offer as he gets older.

Your Daredevil does not understand why his world is slowing down. Owners must make their dogs' transition into their golden years as pleasant and rewarding as possible.

## WHAT TO DO WHEN THE TIME COMES

You are never fully prepared to make a rational decision about putting your dog to sleep. It is very obvious that you love your Irish Terrier or you would not be reading this book. Putting a beloved dog to sleep is extremely difficult. It is a decision that must be made with your vet. You are usually forced to make the decision when your dog experiences one or more life-threatening symptoms that have become serious enough for you to seek veterinary assistance.

If the prognosis of the malady indicates that the end is near and that your beloved pet will only continue to suffer and experience no enjoyment for the balance of his life, then euthanasia is the right choice.

### WHAT IS EUTHANASIA?

Euthanasia derives from the Greek, meaning *good death*. In other words, it means the planned, painless killing of a dog

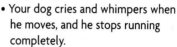

**NOTICING THE SYMPTOMS**
The symptoms listed below are symptoms that gradually appear and become more noticeable. They are not life-threatening; however, the symptoms below are to be taken very seriously and warrant a discussion with your vet:
• Your dog cries and whimpers when he moves, and he stops running completely.
• Convulsions start or become more serious and frequent. The usual convulsion (spasm) is when the dog stiffens and starts to tremble, being unable or unwilling to move. The seizure usually lasts for 5 to 30 minutes.
• Your dog drinks more water and urinates more frequently. Wetting and bowel accidents take place indoors without warning.
• Vomiting becomes more and more frequent.

suffering from a painful, incurable condition, or who is so aged that he cannot walk, see, eat or control his excretory functions. Euthanasia is usually accomplished by injection with an overdose of anesthesia or a barbiturate. Aside from the prick of the needle, the experience is usually painless.

### MAKING THE DECISION

The decision to euthanize your dog is never easy. The days during which the dog becomes ill and the

## COPING WITH LOSS

When your dog dies, you may be as upset as when a human companion passes away. You are losing your protector, your baby, your confidante and your best friend. Many people experience not only grief but also feelings of guilt and doubt as to whether they did all that they could for their pet. Allow yourself to grieve and mourn, and seek help from friends and support groups. You may also wish to consult books and websites that deal with this topic.

end occurs can be unusually stressful for you. If this is your first experience with the death of a loved one, you may need the comfort dictated by your religious beliefs. If you are the head of the family and have children, you should have involved them in the decision of putting your Irish Terrier to sleep. Usually your dog can be maintained on drugs for a few days in order to give you ample time to make a decision. During this time, talking with members of your family or with people who have lived through the same experience can ease the burden of your inevitable decision.

**Consult your vet to help you find a pet cemetery in your area.**

## THE FINAL RESTING PLACE

Dogs can have some of the same privileges as humans. The remains of your beloved dog can be buried in a pet cemetery, which is generally expensive. If your dog has died at home, he can be buried in your yard in a spot marked with a stone or a newly planted bush or tree. Alternatively, your dog can be cremated individually and the ashes returned to you. A less expensive option is mass cremation, although, of course, the ashes cannot then be returned. Vets can usually arrange the cremation on your behalf or can help you locate a pet cemetery in your area. The cost of these options should always be discussed frankly and openly with your vet.

## GETTING ANOTHER DOG?

The grief of losing your beloved dog will be as lasting as the grief of losing a human friend or relative. In most cases, if your dog died of old age (if there is such a thing), he had slowed down considerably. Do you want a new Irish Terrier puppy to replace him? Or are you better off

Pet cemetaries often have areas to display urns in which are contained the ashes of cremated pets.

finding a more mature Irish Terrier, say two to three years of age, which will usually be house-trained and will have an already developed personality. In this case, you can find out if you like each other after a few hours of being together.

The decision is, of course, your own. Do you want another Irish Terrier or perhaps a different breed so as to avoid comparison with your beloved friend? Most people usually buy the same breed because they know (and love) the characteristics of that breed. Then, too, they often know people who have the same breed and perhaps they are lucky enough that a breeder that they know and respect expects a litter soon. What could be better?

## TO THE RESCUE

Some people choose to adopt or "rescue" an older dog instead of buying a new puppy. Some older dogs may have come from abusive environments and be fearful, while other dogs may have developed many bad habits; both situations can present challenges to their new owners. Training an older dog will take more time and patience, but persistence and an abundance of praise and love can transform a dog into a well-behaved, loyal companion.

When you purchase your Irish Terrier, you will make it clear to the breeder whether you want one just as a lovable companion and pet, or if you hope to be buying an Irish Terrier with show prospects. No reputable breeder will sell you a young puppy and tell you that it is *definitely* of show quality, for so much can go wrong during the early months of a puppy's development. If you plan to show, what you will hopefully have acquired is a puppy with "show potential."

To the novice, exhibiting an Irish Terrier in the show ring may look easy, but it takes a lot of hard work and devotion to do top winning at a show such as the prestigious Westminster Kennel Club dog show or Crufts dog show, not to mention a little luck, too!

The first concept that the canine novice learns when watching a dog show is that each dog first competes against members of his own breed. Once the judge has selected the best member of each breed (Best of Breed), provided that the show is judged on a Group system, that chosen dog will compete with other dogs in his group. Finally, the dogs chosen first in each group will compete for Best in Show.

The second concept that you must understand is that the dogs are not actually compared against one another. The judge compares each dog against his breed standard, the written description of the ideal specimen that is approved by the American Kennel Club (AKC) or another national

## CLUB CONTACTS

You can get information about dog shows from the national kennel clubs:

American Kennel Club
5580 Centerview Dr.
Raleigh, NC 27606-3390 USA
www.akc.org

Canadian Kennel Club
89 Skyway Ave., Suite 100, Etobicoke, Ontario
M9W 6R4 Canada
www.ckc.ca

The Kennel Club
1-5 Clarges St.
Piccadilly, London W1Y 8AB, UK
www.the-kennel-club.org.uk

Fédération Cynologique Internationale
14, rue Leopold II, B-6530 Thuin, Belgium
www.fci.be

club. While some early breed standards were indeed based on specific dogs that were famous or popular, many dedicated enthusiasts say that a perfect specimen, as described in the standard, has never walked into a show ring, has never been bred and, to the woe of dog breeders around the globe, does not exist. Breeders attempt to get as close to this ideal as possible with every litter, but theoretically the "perfect" dog is so elusive that it is impossible. (And if the "perfect" dog were born, breeders and judges would never agree that it was indeed "perfect.")

If you are interested in exploring the world of dog showing, your best bet is to join your local breed club or the national parent club, which is the Irish Terrier Club of America. These clubs often host both regional and national specialties, shows only for Irish Terriers, which can include conformation as well as obedience and field trials. Even if you have no intention of competing with your Irish Terrier, a specialty is like a festival for lovers of the breed who congregate to share their favorite topic: Irish Terriers! Clubs also send out newsletters, and some organize training days and seminars in order that people may learn more about their chosen breed.

To locate the breed club closest to you, contact the American

The Best of Breed winner at the UK's prestigious Crufts show competes in the Group ring.

Kennel Club, which furnishes the rules and regulations for all of these events plus general dog registration and other basic requirements of dog ownership.

In the US, the American Kennel Club offers three kinds of conformation shows: An all-breed show (for all AKC-recognized breeds), a specialty show (for one breed only, usually sponsored by the parent club) and a Group show (for all breeds in the Group).

For a dog to become an AKC champion of record, the dog must accumulate 15 points at the shows from at least three different judges, including two "majors." A "major" is defined as a three-, four- or five-point win, and the number of points per win is determined by the number of dogs entered in the show on that day. Depending on the breed, the number of points that are awarded varies. More popular breeds require more dogs entered to rack up points; less popular breeds require less dogs entered.

At any dog show, only one dog and one bitch of each breed can win points. Dog showing does not offer "co-ed" classes. Dogs and bitches never compete against each other in the classes. Non-champion dogs are called "class dogs" because they compete in one of five classes. Dogs are entered in a particular class depending on their age and previous show wins. To begin, there is the Puppy Class (for 6- to 9-

> **TEMPERAMENT PLUS**
> Although it seems that physical conformation is the only factor considered in the show ring, temperament is also of utmost importance. An aggressive or fearful dog should not be shown, as bad behavior will not be tolerated and may pose a threat to the judge, other exhibitors, you and your dog.

month-olds and for 9- to 12-month-olds); this class is followed by the Novice Class (for dogs that have not won any first prizes except in the Puppy Class or three first prizes in the Novice Class and have not accumulated any points toward their champion title); the Bred-by-Exhibitor Class (for dogs handled by their breeders or handled by one of the breeder's immediate family); the American-bred Class (for dogs bred in the US) and the Open Class (for any dog that is not a champion).

The judge at the show begins judging the Puppy Class, first dogs and then bitches, and proceeds through the classes. The judge places his winners first through fourth in each class. In the Winners Class, the first-place winners of each class compete with one another to determine Winners Dog and Winners Bitch. The judge also places a Reserve Winners Dog and Reserve Winners Bitch, which could be awarded

the points in the case of a disqualification. The Winners Dog and Winners Bitch are the two that are awarded the points for the breed, then compete with any champions of record entered in the show. The judge reviews the Winners Dog, Winners Bitch and all of the other champions to select his Best of Breed. The Best of Winners is selected between the Winners Dog and Winners Bitch. Were one of these two to be selected Best of Breed, it would automatically be named Best of Winners as well. Finally the judge selects his Best of Opposite Sex to the Best of Breed winner.

At a Group show or all-breed show, the Best of Breed winners from each breed then compete against one another for Group One through Group Four. The judge compares each Best of Breed to his breed standard, and the dog that most closely lives up to the ideal for his breed is selected as Group One. Finally, all seven group winners (from the Terrier Group, Toy Group, Hound Group, etc.) compete for Best in Show.

To find out about dog shows in your area, you can subscribe to the American Kennel Club's monthly magazine, the *American Kennel Gazette* and the accompanying *Events Calendar*. You can also look in your local newspaper for advertisements for dog shows in your area or go on the Internet to the AKC's website, www.akc.org.

If your Irish Terrier is six months of age or older and registered with the AKC, you can enter him in a dog show where the breed is offered classes. Provided that your Irish Terrier does not have a disqualifying fault, he can compete. Only unaltered dogs can be entered in a dog show, so if you have spayed or neutered your Irish Terrier, you cannot compete in conformation shows. The reason for this is simple. Dog shows are the main forum to prove which representatives in a breed are worthy of being bred. Only dogs that have achieved championships—the AKC "seal of approval" for quality in pure-bred dogs—should be bred. Altered dogs, however, can participate in other AKC events such as obedience trials, instinct tests and the Canine Good Citizen program.

Before you actually step into the ring, you would be well advised to sit back and observe the judge's ring procedure. If it is your first time in the ring, do not be over-anxious and run to the front of the line. It is much better to stand back and study how the

## AKC GROUPS

For showing purposes, the American Kennel Club divides its recognized breeds into seven groups: Sporting Dogs, Hounds, Working Dogs, Terriers, Toys, Non-Sporting Dogs and Herding Dogs.

exhibitor in front of you is performing. The judge asks each handler to "stack" the dog, hopefully showing the dog off to his best advantage. The judge will observe the dog from a distance and from different angles, and approach the dog to check his teeth, overall structure, alertness and muscle tone, as well as consider how well the dog "conforms" to the standard. Most importantly, the judge will have the exhibitor move the dog around the ring in some pattern that he should specify (another advantage to not going first, but always listen since some judges change their directions—and the judge is always right!). Finally, the judge will give the dog one last look before moving on to the next exhibitor.

If you are not in the top four in your class at your first show, do not be discouraged. Be patient and consistent, and you may eventually find yourself in a winning line-up. Remember that the winners were once in your shoes and have devoted many hours and much money to earn the placement. If you find that your dog is losing every time and never getting a nod, it may be time to consider a different dog sport or to just enjoy your Irish Terrier as a pet. Parent clubs offer other events, such as agility, terrier trials, tracking, obedience events, instinct tests and more, which may be of interest to the owner of a well-trained Irish Terrier.

**OBEDIENCE TRIALS**

Obedience trials in the US trace back to the early 1930s, when organized obedience training was developed to demonstrate how well dog and owner could work together. The pioneer of obedience trials is Mrs. Helen Whitehouse Walker, a Standard Poodle fancier, who designed a series of exercises after the Associated Sheep, Police Army Dog Society of Great Britain. Since the days of Mrs. Walker, obedience trials have grown by leaps and bounds, and today there are over 2,000 trials held in the US every year, with more than 100,000 dogs competing. Any registered AKC dog can enter an obedience trial, regardless of conformational disqualifications or neutering.

Obedience trials are divided into three levels of progressive difficulty. At the first level, the Novice, dogs compete for the title Companion Dog (CD); at the intermediate level, the Open, dogs compete for the title Companion Dog Excellent (CDX); and at the advanced level, the Utility, dogs compete for the title Utility Dog (UD). Classes are sub-divided into "A" (for beginners) and "B" (for more experienced handlers). A

## A GENTLEMAN'S SPORT

Whether or not your dog wins top honors, showing is a pleasant social event. Sometimes, one may meet a troublemaker or nasty exhibitor, but these people should be ignored and forgotten. In the extremely rare case that someone threatens or harasses you or your dog, you can lodge a complaint with the hosting kennel club. This should be done with extreme prudence. Complaints are investigated seriously and should never be filed on a whim.

The judge examines each dog physically, including the mouth and teeth. The dog must tolerate such handling and never snap at the judge or otherwise act aggressively.

perfect score at any level is 200, and a dog must score 170 or better to earn a "leg," of which three are needed to earn the title. To earn points, the dog must score more than 50% of the available points in each exercise; the possible points range from 20 to 40.

Each level consists of a different set of exercises. In the Novice level, the dog must heel on- and off-leash, come, long sit, long down and stand for examination. These skills are the basic ones required for a well-behaved "Companion Dog." The Open level requires that the dog perform the same exercises above but without a leash for extended lengths of time, as well as retrieve a dumbbell, broad jump and drop on recall. In the Utility level, dogs must perform ten difficult exercises, including scent discrimination, hand signals for basic commands, directed jump and directed retrieve.

Once a dog has earned the UD title, he can compete with other proven obedience dogs for the coveted title of Utility Dog Excellent (UDX), which requires that the dog win "legs" in ten shows. Utility Dogs who earn "legs" in Open B and Utility B earn points toward their Obedience Trial Champion title. In 1977, the title Obedience Trial Champion (OTCh.) was established by the AKC. To become an OTCh., a dog needs to earn 100 points, which requires three first places in Open B and Utility under three different judges.

The Grand Prix of obedience trials, the AKC National Obedience Invitational gives qualifying Utility Dogs the chance to win the newest and highest title: National Obedience Champion (NOC). Only the top 25 ranked obedience dogs, plus any dog ranked in the top 3 in his breed, are allowed to compete.

**TRACKING**
Any dog is capable of tracking, using his nose to follow a trail. Tracking tests are exciting and competitive ways to test your Irish Terrier's ability to search and rescue. The AKC started tracking tests in 1937, when the first AKC-licensed test took place as part of the Utility level at an obedience trial. Ten years later in 1947, the AKC offered the first title, Tracking Dog (TD). It was not until 1980 that the AKC added the title Tracking Dog Excellent (TDX), which was followed by the title Versatile Surface Tracking (VST) in 1995. The title Champion Tracker (CT) is awarded to a dog who has earned all three titles.

In the beginning level of tracking, the owner follows the dog through a field on a long leash. To earn the TD title, the dog must follow a track laid by a human 30 to 120 minutes prior. The track is about 500 yards long with up to 5 directional changes. The TDX requires that the dog follow a track that is 3 to 5 hours old over a course up to 1,000 yards long with up to 7 directional changes. The VST requires that the dog follow a track up to 5 hours old through an urban setting.

### AGILITY TRIALS
Having had its origins in the UK back in 1977, AKC agility had its official beginning in the US in August 1994, when the first licensed agility trials were held. The AKC allows all registered breeds (including Miscellaneous Class breeds) to participate, providing the dog is 12 months of age or older. Agility is designed so that the handler demonstrates how well the dog can work at his side. The handler directs his dog over an obstacle course that includes jumps as well as tires, the dog walk, weave poles, pipe tunnels, collapsed tunnels, etc. While working their way through the course, the dog must keep one eye and ear on the handler and the rest of his body on the course. The handler gives verbal and hand signals to guide the dog through the course. Again, it is of utmost importance for the Irish Terrier to be reliably trained and for the handler to have full control over the dog while running through the

What a delight when an owner has a faithful canine companion with whom he can share the excitement—and hopefully the successes—of the show ring.

course to prevent scuffles with other competitors.

The first organization to promote agility trials in the US was the United States Dog Agility Association, Inc. (USDAA), which was established in 1986 and spawned numerous member clubs around the country. Both the USDAA and the AKC offer titles to winning dogs.

Agility is great fun for dog and owner, with many rewards for everyone involved. Interested owners should join a training club that has obstacles and experienced agility handlers who can introduce you and your dog to the "ropes" (and tires, tunnels, etc.).

As an Irish Terrier owner, you have selected your dog so that you and your loved ones can have a companion, a protector, a hunter and a four-legged family member. You invest time, money and effort to care for and train the family's new charge. Of course, this chosen canine behaves perfectly! Well, perfectly like a *dog*.

### THINK LIKE A DOG

Dogs do not think like humans, nor do humans think like dogs, though we try. Unfortunately, a dog is incapable of comprehending how humans think, so the responsibility falls on the owner to adopt a viable canine mindset. Dogs cannot rationalize and they exist in the present moment. Many a dog owner makes the mistake in training of thinking that he can reprimand his dog for something that the dog did a while ago. Basically, you cannot even reprimand a dog for something he did 20 seconds ago! Either catch him in the act or forget it! It is a waste of your and your dog's time—in his mind, you are reprimanding him for whatever he is doing at that moment.

The following behavioral problems represent some which owners most commonly encounter. Every dog is unique and every situation is unique. No author could purport for you to solve your Irish Terrier's problems simply by reading a chapter in a breed book. Here we outline some basic "dogspeak" so that owners' chances of solving behavioral problems are increased.

Discuss bad habits with your vet and he can recommend a behavioral specialist to consult in appropriate cases. Since behavioral abnormalities are the main reason for owners' abandoning their pets, we hope that you will make a valiant effort to solve your Irish Terrier's problems. Patience and understanding are virtues that must dwell in every pet-loving household.

### AGGRESSION

This is a problem that concerns all responsible dog owners. Aggression can be a very big problem in dogs, and, when not controlled, always becomes dangerous. An aggressive dog, no matter the size, may lunge at, bite or even attack a person or another dog. Aggressive behavior is not to be tolerated. It is more than just inappropriate behavior; it is painful for a family to watch their dog become unpredictable in his behavior to the point where they are afraid of him. While not all aggressive behavior is dangerous, things like growling, baring teeth, etc., can be frightening. It is important to ascertain why the dog is acting in this manner. Aggression is a display of dominance, and the dog should not have the dominant role in his pack, which is, in this case, your family.

It is important not to challenge an aggressive dog, as this could provoke an attack. Observe your Irish Terrier's body language. Does he make direct eye contact and stare? Does he try to make himself as large as possible: ears pricked, chest out, tail erect? Height and size signify authority in a dog pack—being taller or "above" another dog literally means that he is "above" in social status. These body signals tell you that your Irish Terrier thinks he is in charge, a problem that needs to be addressed. An aggressive dog is unpredictable; you never know when he is going to strike and what he is going to do. You cannot understand why a dog that is playful one minute is growling the next.

Fear is a common cause of aggression in dogs. Perhaps your Irish had a negative experience as a puppy, which causes him to be fearful when a similar situation presents itself later in life. The dog may act aggressively in order to protect himself from whatever

## BELLY UP!

When two dogs are introduced, they will naturally establish who is dominant. This may involve one dog placing his front paws on the other's shoulders, or one dog rolling over and exposing his belly, thereby assuming a submissive status. If neither dog submits, they may fight until one has been pinned down. This behavior can be upsetting for owners to watch, especially if your dog takes one look and throws himself on the ground. The biggest mistake you can make is to interfere, pulling on the leashes and confusing the dogs. If you don't allow them to establish their pecking order, you undermine the pack mentality, which can cause your dog great stress. If you separate dogs in the middle of a fight, the interference may incite them to attack each other viciously. Your best choice is to stay out of it!

is making him afraid. It is not always easy to determine what is making your dog fearful, but if you can isolate what brings out the fear reaction, you can help the dog get over it.

Supervise your Irish Terrier's interactions with people and other dogs, and praise the dog when it goes well. If he starts to act aggressively in a situation, correct him and remove him from the situation. Do not let people approach the dog and start petting him without your express permission. That way, you can have the dog sit to accept petting, and praise him when he behaves properly. You are focusing on praise and on modifying his behavior by rewarding him when he acts appropriately. By being gentle and by supervising his interactions, you are showing him that there is no need to be afraid or defensive.

The best solution is to consult a behavioral specialist, one who has experience with terriers, specifically the Irish if possible. Together, perhaps you can pinpoint the cause of your dog's aggression and do something about it. An aggressive dog cannot be trusted, and a dog that cannot be trusted is not safe to have as a family pet. If, very unusually, you find that your pet has become untrustworthy and you feel it necessary to seek a new home with a more suitable family and environment, explain fully to the new owners all your reasons for rehoming the dog to be fair to all concerned. In the *very worst* case, you will have to consider euthanasia.

**AGGRESSION TOWARD OTHER DOGS**
The male Irish Terrier does have the tendency to be dog-aggressive, and males and females alike can be aggressive toward members of their own sex. A dog's aggressive behavior toward another dog stems from not enough exposure to other dogs at an early age. Therefore, you need to make a concerted effort when your Irish is young to properly socialize him with other dogs to minimize the risk of problems as an adult.

If other dogs make your Irish Terrier nervous and agitated, he will lash out as a protective mechanism. A dog that has not received sufficient exposure to

**TUG-OF-WAR**
You should never play tug-of-war games with your puppy. Such games create a struggle for "top dog" position and teach the puppy that it is okay to challenge you. It will also encourage your puppy's natural tendency to bite down hard and *win*.

other canines tends to think that he is the only dog on the planet. The animal becomes so dominant that he does not even show signs that he is fearful or threatened. Without growling or any other physical signal as a warning, he will lunge at and bite the other dog.

A way to correct this is to let your Irish Terrier approach another dog when walking on leash. Watch very closely and, at the first sign of aggression, correct your Irish Terrier and pull him away. Scold him for any sign of discomfort, and then praise him when he ignores the other dog. Keep this up until either he stops the aggressive behavior, learns to ignore other dogs or even accepts other dogs. Praise him lavishly for his correct behavior.

### DOMINANT AGGRESSION

A social hierarchy is firmly established in a wild dog pack. The dog wants to dominate those under him and please those above him. Dogs know that there must be a leader. If you are not the obvious choice for emperor, the dog will assume the throne! These conflicting innate desires are what a dog owner is up against when he sets about training a dog. In training a dog to obey commands, the owner is reinforcing that he is the top dog in the "pack" and that the dog should, and should want to, serve his superior. Thus, the

Feeding time is a good time to reinforce basic commands and good behavior. Get in the routine of having your Irish sit at mealtime and wait for your "OK" before chowing down.

owner is suppressing the dog's urge to dominate by modifying his behavior and making him obedient.

An important part of training is taking every opportunity to reinforce that you are the leader. The simple action of making your Irish Terrier sit to wait for his food instead of allowing him to run up to get it when he wants it says that you control when he eats; he is dependent on you for food. Although it may be difficult, do not give in to your dog's wishes every time he whines at you or looks at you with pleading eyes. It is a constant effort to show the dog that his place in the pack is at the bottom.

This is not meant to sound cruel or inhumane. You love your Irish Terrier and you should treat him with care and affection. You (hopefully) did not get a dog just so you could control another creature. Dog training is not about being cruel, it is about molding the dog's behavior into what is acceptable and teaching him to live by your rules. In theory, it is quite simple: catch him in appropriate behavior and reward him for it. Add a dog into the equation and it becomes a bit more trying, but, as a rule of thumb, positive reinforcement is what works best.

With a dominant dog, punishment and negative reinforcement can have the opposite effect of what you are after. It can make a dog fearful and/or act out aggressively if he feels he is being challenged. Remember, a dominant dog perceives himself at the top of the social heap and will fight to defend his perceived status. The best way to prevent that is to never give him reason to think that he is in control in the first place.

If you are having trouble training your Irish Terrier and it

> **DOMINANT AGGRESSION**
> Never allow your puppy to growl at you or bare his tiny teeth. Such behavior is dominant and aggressive. If not corrected, the dog will repeat the behavior, which will become more threatening as he grows larger and will eventually lead to biting.

seems as if he is constantly challenging your authority, seek the help of an obedience trainer or behavioral specialist. A professional will work with both you and your dog to teach you effective techniques to use at home. Beware of trainers who rely on excessively harsh methods; scolding is necessary now and then, but the focus in your training should *always* be on positive reinforcement.

### SEPARATION ANXIETY

Recognized by behaviorists as the most common form of stress for dogs, separation anxiety can also lead to destructive behaviors in your dog. It's more than your Irish Terrier's howling his displeasure at your leaving the house and his being left alone. This is a normal reaction, no different than the child who cries as his mother leaves him on the first day at school. Separation anxiety is more serious. In fact, if you are constantly with your dog, he will come to expect you with him all of the time, making it even more traumatic for him when you are not there.

Obviously, you enjoy spending time with your dog, and he thrives on your love and attention. However, it should not become a dependent relationship in which he is heartbroken without you. This broken heart can also bring on destructive behavior as well as loss of appetite, depression and lack of interest in play and interaction. Canine behaviorists have been spending much time and energy to help owners better understand the significance of this stressful condition.

One thing you can do to minimize separation anxiety is to make your entrances and exits as low-key as possible. Do not give your dog a long drawn-out goodbye, and do not lavish him with hugs and kisses when you return. This is giving in to the attention that he craves, and it will only

Separation anxiety is very common in dogs today, and many dogs eagerly anticipate their owners' arrival home from a long day at work.

## I'M HOME!

Dogs left alone for varying lengths of time may often react wildly when their owners return. Sometimes they run, jump, bite, chew, tear things apart, wet themselves, gobble their food or behave in very undisciplined ways. If your dog behaves in this manner upon your return home, allow him to calm down before greeting him or he will consider your attention as a reward for his antics.

make him miss it more when you are away. Another thing you can try is to give your dog a treat when you leave; this will not only keep him occupied and keep his mind off the fact that you have just left, but it will also help him associate your leaving with a pleasant experience.

You may have to accustom your dog to being left alone in intervals. Of course, when your dog starts whimpering as you approach the door, your first instinct will be to run to him and comfort him, but do not do it!

### THE MIGHTY MALE

Males, whether castrated or not, will mount almost anything: a pillow, your leg or, much to your dismay, even your neighbor's leg. As with other types of inappropriate behavior, the dog must be corrected while in the act, which for once is not difficult. Often he will not let go! While a puppy is experimenting with his very first urges, his owners feel he needs to "sow his oats" and allow the pup to mount. As the pup grows into a full-size dog, with full-size urges, it becomes a nuisance and an embarrassment. Males always appear as if they are trying to "save the race," more determined and stronger than imaginable. While altering the dog at an appropriate age will limit the dog's desire, it usually does not remove it entirely.

Eventually he will adjust to your absence. His anxiety stems from being placed in an unfamiliar situation; by familiarizing him with being alone, he will learn that he will be fine without you near. That is not to say you should purposely leave your dog home alone, but the dog needs to know that, while he can depend on you for his care, you do not have to be by his side 24 hours a day. Some behaviorists recommend tiring the dog out before you leave home—take him for a good long walk or engage in a game of fetch.

When the dog is alone in the house, he should be placed in his crate—another distinct advantage to crate training your dog. The crate should be placed in his familiar happy family area, where he normally sleeps and already feels comfortable, thereby making him feel more at ease when he is alone. Be sure to give the dog a special chew toy to enjoy while he settles into his crate.

### SEXUAL BEHAVIOR

Dogs exhibit certain sexual behaviors that may have influenced your choice of male or female when you first purchased your Irish Terrier. To a certain extent, spaying/neutering will eliminate these behaviors, but if you are purchasing a dog that you wish to breed from, you should be aware of what you will have to deal with throughout the dog's life.

Female dogs usually have two estruses per year, with each season lasting about three weeks. These are the only times in which a female dog will mate, and she usually will not allow this until the second week of the cycle, although this varies from bitch to bitch. If not bred during the heat cycle, it is not uncommon for a bitch to experience a false pregnancy, in which her mammary glands swell and she exhibits maternal tendencies toward toys or other objects.

With male dogs, owners must be aware that whole dogs (dogs who are not neutered) have the natural inclination to mark their territory. Males mark their territory by spraying small amounts of urine as they lift their legs in a macho ritual. Marking can occur both outdoors in the yard and around the neighborhood as well as indoors on furniture legs, curtains and the sofa. Such behavior can be very frustrating for the owner; early training is strongly urged before the "urge" strikes your dog. Neutering the male at an appropriate early age can solve this problem before it becomes a habit.

Other problems associated with males are wandering and mounting. Both of these habits, of course, belong to the unneutered dog, whose sexual drive leads him away from home in search of the bitch in heat. Males will mount females in heat, as well as any other dog, male or female, that happens to catch their fancy. Other possible mounting partners include his owner, the furniture, guests to the home and strangers on the street. Discourage such behavior early on.

Owners must further recognize that mounting is not merely a sexual expression but also one of dominance, seen in males and females alike. Be consistent and be persistent, and you will find that you can "move mounters."

**CHEWING**
The national canine pastime is chewing! Every dog loves to sink his "canines" into a tasty bone, so it is important to provide your dog with appropriate chew toys so that he doesn't destroy your possessions or make a habit of gnawing on your hands and fingers. Dogs need to chew to massage their gums, to make their new teeth feel better and to exercise their jaws. This is a natural behavior that is deeply embedded in all things canine. Your role as owner is not to stop the dog's chewing, but rather to redirect it to positive, chew-worthy objects.

Be an informed owner and purchase safe chew toys, like strong nylon bones, that will not splinter. Since each Irish Terrier seems to have his own preference for toys, provide your Irish with toys that keep him engaged and interested. Be sure that the objects are safe and durable, since your dog's safety is at risk. Again, the owner is responsible for ensuring a dog-proof environment.

The best answer is prevention; that is, put your shoes, handbags and other tasty objects in their proper places (out of the reach of the growing canine mouth). Direct puppies to their toys whenever you see them "tasting" the furniture legs or the leg of your pants. Make a loud noise to attract the pup's attention and immediately escort him to his chew toy and engage him with the toy for at least four minutes, praising and encouraging him all the while. An array of safe, interesting chew toys will keep your dog's mind and teeth occupied, and distracted from chewing on things he shouldn't.

Some trainers recommend deterrents, such as hot pepper, a bitter spice or a product designed for this purpose, to discourage the dog from chewing unwanted objects. Test these products to see which works best before investing in large quantities.

### DIGGING

Digging, which is seen as a destructive behavior to humans, is actually quite a natural behavior in dogs. Terriers (the "earthdogs"), like your Irish Terrier, are most closely associated with digging,

**SOUND BITES**

When a dog bites, there is always a good reason for his doing so. Many dogs are trained to protect a person, an area or an object. When that person, area or object is violated, the dog will attack. A dog attacks with his mouth. He has no other means of attack.

Fighting dogs (and there are many breeds that fight) are taught to fight, but they also have a natural instinct to fight. This instinct is normally reserved for other dogs, though unfortunate accidents can occur; for example, when a baby crawls toward a fighting dog and the dog mistakes the crawling child as a potential attacker.

If a dog is a biter for seemingly no reason, if he bites the hand that feeds him or if he snaps at members of your family, see your vet or behaviorist immediately to learn how to modify the dog's behavior.

and a terrier doesn't need much persuasion to get his paws dirty!

Any dog's desire to dig can be irrepressible and most frustrating to his owners, and it can be dangerous to the dog if he tries to "escape" by digging under a fence. When digging occurs in your garden, it is actually a normal behavior redirected into something the dog can do in his everyday life. In the wild, a dog would be actively seeking food, making his own shelter, etc. He would be using his paws in a purposeful manner for his survival. Since you provide him with food and shelter, he has no need to use his paws for these purposes, so the energy that he would be using may manifest itself in the form of little holes all over your yard and flower beds.

Perhaps your dog is digging as a reaction to boredom—it is somewhat similar to someone eating a whole bag of chips in front of the TV—because they are there and there is nothing better to do! Basically, the answer is to provide the dog with adequate play and exercise so that his mind and paws are occupied, and so that he feels as if he is doing something useful.

Of course, digging is easiest to control if it is stopped as soon as possible, but it is often hard to catch a dog in the act. If your dog is a compulsive digger and is not easily distracted by other activities, you can designate an area on your property where he is allowed to dig. If you catch him digging in an off-limits area of the yard, immediately take him to the approved area and praise him for digging there. Keep a close eye on him so that you can catch him in the act—that is the only way to make him understand what is permitted and what is not. If you take him to a hole he dug an hour ago and tell him "No," he will

understand that you are not fond of holes, dirt or flowers. If you catch him while he is stifle-deep in your tulips, that is when he will get your message.

## JUMPING UP

Jumping up is a dog's friendly way of saying hello! Some dog owners do not mind when their dog jumps up. The problem arises when guests come to the house and the dog greets them in the same manner—whether they like it or not! However friendly the greeting may be, the chances are that your visitors will not appreciate your dog's enthusiasm. The dog will not be able to distinguish upon whom he can jump and whom he cannot. Therefore, it is probably best to discourage this behavior entirely.

Pick a command such as "Off" (avoid using "Down" since you will use that for

**NO JUMPING**
Stop a dog from jumping up before he jumps. If he is getting ready to jump onto you, simply walk away. If he jumps up on you before you can turn away, lift your knee so that it bumps him in the chest. Do not be forceful. Your dog soon will realize that jumping up is not a productive way of getting attention.

Where there's dirt, there's a terrier! It's not uncommon to find an earthdog among the flowers, paws poised to dig in.

the dog to lie down) and tell him "Off" when he jumps up. Place him on the ground on all fours and have him sit, praising him the whole time. Always lavish him with praise and petting when he is in the sit position. In this way, you can give him a warm affectionate greeting, let him know that you are as pleased to see him as he is to see you and instill good manners at the same time!

## BARKING

Dogs cannot talk—oh, what they would say if they could! Instead, barking is a dog's way of "talking." It can be somewhat frustrating because it is not always easy to tell what a dog means by his bark—is he excited, happy, frightened or angry? Whatever it is that the dog is trying to say, he should not be punished for barking. It is only when the barking becomes excessive, and when the excessive barking becomes a bad habit, that the behavior needs to be modified.

Fortunately, Irish Terriers are not noisy. Their barking generally is limited to warning or alerting their owners of something or someone. If an intruder came into your home in the middle of the night and your Irish Terrier barked a warning, wouldn't you be pleased? You would probably deem your dog a hero, a wonderful guardian and protector of the home. On the other hand, if a friend drops by unexpectedly,

rings the doorbell and is greeted with sudden sharp barking, you would probably be annoyed at the dog. But in reality, isn't this just the same behavior? The dog does not know any better. Unless he sees who is at the door and it is someone he knows, he will bark as a means of vocalizing that his (and your) territory is being threatened. While your friend is not posing a threat, it is all the same to the dog. Barking is his means of letting you know that there is an intrusion, whether friend or foe, on your property. This type of barking is instinctive and should not be discouraged.

Excessive habitual barking, however, is a problem that

### QUIET ON THE SET

To encourage proper barking, you can teach your dog the command "Quiet." When someone comes to the door and the dog barks a few times, praise him. Talk to him soothingly and, when he stops barking, tell him "Quiet" and continue to praise him. In this sense, you are letting him bark his warning, which is an instinctive behavior, and then rewarding him for being quiet after a few barks. You may initially reward him with a treat after he has been quiet for a few minutes.

This "nosy" Irish is looking for a treat. Curiosity and the love of food mean that any interesting tidbits within a dog's reach are likely to be investigated (and stolen).

stranger, the frantic one meant to terrify a cat, the happy one welcoming a family member, etc. It is similar to a person's tone of voice, except that the dog has to rely totally on tone of voice.

**FOOD STEALING**

Is your dog devising ways of stealing food from your coffee table or kitchen counter? If so, you must answer the following questions: Is your Irish Terrier a bit hungry, or is he "constantly famished" like many dogs seem to be? Face it, some dogs are more food-motivated than others. They are totally obsessed by the smell of food and can only think of their next meal. Food stealing is terrific fun and always yields a great reward—FOOD, glorious food.

Your goal as an owner, therefore, is to be sensible about where food is placed in the home and to reprimand your dog whenever he is caught in the act of stealing. But remember, only reprimand your dog if you actually see him stealing, not later when the crime is discovered; that will be of no use at all and will only serve to confuse him.

should be corrected early on. As your Irish Terrier grows up, you will be able to tell when his barking is purposeful and when it is for no reason. You soon will learn to distinguish your dog's different barks—the bark that signals a

**BEGGING**

Just like food stealing, begging is a favorite pastime of hungry puppies! It achieves that same tasty result—FOOD! Dogs quickly learn that their owners keep the "good food" for themselves, and that we humans do not dine on dry food alone. Begging is a conditioned response related to a specific stimulus, time and place. The sounds of the kitchen, cans and bottles opening, crinkling bags, the smell of food in preparation, etc., will excite the dog, and soon the paws will be in the air!

Here is the solution to stopping this behavior: Never give in to a beggar! You are rewarding the dog for sitting pretty, jumping up, whining and rubbing his nose into you by giving him food. By ignoring the dog, you will (eventually) force the behavior into extinction. Note that the behavior is likely to get worse before it disappears, so be sure there are not any "softies" in the family who will give in to little "Oliver" every time he whimpers, "More, please."

## COPROPHAGIA

Feces eating is, to humans, one of the most disgusting behaviors that our dogs could engage in; yet, to dogs, it is perfectly normal. It is hard for us to understand why a dog would want to eat his own feces. He could be seeking certain nutrients that are missing from his diet, he could be just hungry or he could be attracted by the pleasing (to a dog) scent. While coprophagia most often refers to the dog's eating his own feces, a dog may just as likely eat that of another animal as well if he comes across it. Dogs often find the stool of cats

and horses more palatable than that of other dogs.

Vets have found that diets with low levels of digestibility, containing relatively low levels of fiber and high levels of starch, increase coprophagia. Therefore, high-fiber diets may decrease the likelihood of dogs' eating feces. Both the consistency of the stool (how firm it feels in the dog's mouth) and the presence of undigested nutrients increase the likelihood. Once the dog develops diarrhea from feces eating, he will likely stop this distasteful habit.

To discourage this behavior, first make sure that the food you are feeding your dog is nutritionally complete and that he is getting enough food. If changes in his diet do not seem to work, and no medical cause can be found, you will have to modify the behavior through environmental control before it becomes a habit. The best way to prevent your dog from eating his stool is to make it unavailable—clean up after he eliminates and remove any stool from the yard. If it is not there, he cannot eat it.

Reprimanding for stool eating rarely impresses the dog. Vets recommend distracting the dog while he is in the act of stool eating. Coprophagia is seen most frequently in pups 6 to 12 months of age, and usually disappears around the dog's first birthday.

# INDEX

Activities 65, 94
Adaptability 28
Adult
—diet 62
—health 103
—training 75
Aggression 24, 28, 55, 142
—dominant 145-146
—toward other dogs 23, 28, 41, 55, 94-95, 141, 144
Agility trials 95
Aging 103, 129-130
Ahtram kennels 18
Air travel 71
All-breed show 135
Allergy
—airborne 105
—food 106
—parasite bite 105
American dog tick **112, 113**
American Kennel Club 18, 134-135, 140-141
—address 134
—breed standard 30
—website 137
*American Kennel Gazette* 137
Ancestors of breed 10, 13
*Ancylostoma caninum* **117**
Antics 28
Aroostock kennels 18
*Ascaris lumbricoides* **116**
Ashe, Edward C 13
Attention 86
Auto-immune illness 105
Axelrod, Dr. Herbert R. 115
Backpacking 95
Badger **10**
Barking 153
Barnett, Mr. C. J. 15, 17
Bathing 67
Bedding 46, 59, 80
Begging 154
Behavioral problems 142
Behavioral specialist 142, 144, 146
Best in Show 134, 137
Best of Breed 134, 137
Best of Opposite Sex 137
Best of Winners 137
Blazer kennels 18
Boarding 72
Body 30
Body language 143
Bolton Woods Mixer 18
Bones 47, 149
Booster immunizations 102
Boredom 65, 151
*Borrelia burgdorferi* 113
Bowls 49
Breda Mixer 18

Breed club 37, 135
—events 95, 135, 138
Breed standard 30, 135
—American Kennel Club 30
Breeder 36-37, 41
—selection 36-37, 42
Brehon Code 9
Brickbat **16**
Britain 10
Brown dog tick **115**
Brushing 66-67
Bull-and-Terrier 12
Burial 133
Cairn Terrier 10
Canada 21
Canadian Kennel Club 134
Cancer 126
Canine cough 102
Canine Good Citizen 137
Car travel 71
Carey, Dr. R. B. 15
Cats 24, 28, 85
Celtic Badger 18
Champion 137
—becoming a 135
—Tracker 140
Chew toys 47, 59, 149-150
—possessiveness with 47
Chewing 50, 59, 81, 149
Children 24-25, 56
Classes at shows 136
Clipping 67
Clyde, Robert 19
Coat 11
Cocksure 19
Cognitive dysfunction syndrome 127
Collar 48, 85
Color 10-11, 14, 16-17, 40
—puppy 38
—purification 16
Colostrum 61
Come 90
Commands 77, 82, 87-93, 151
Companion Dog 139-140
Companion Dog Excellent 139
Conformation 30
Control 77, 80
Coprophagia 155
Coronavirus 102
Crate 45-46, 58-59, 71-72, 148
—safety 50
—training 45, 46, 76-84, 148
Cremation 133
Cruft, Charles 17
Crying 53, 58
*Ctenocephalides* **110**
*Ctenocephalides canis* **108**
Daredevil 11, 13
Deer tick **113**

Dental care 103
Dental health 99
*Dermacentor variabilis* **112, 113**
Destructive behavior 65, 81, 130, 146, 149-150
Dewclaw removal 40
Diet 60, 106
—adult 62
—grain-based 63
—puppy 61
—senior 63, 103, 130
Digging 51, 150
*Dipylidium caninum* 118
*Dirofilaria immitis* **121**
Discipline 81, 84
Distemper 101, 102
Docking tails 40
Dog-aggression 23, 41, 55, 94-95, 141, 144
Dog flea **108**
*Dog in Health and Disease, The* 10, 13
Dog tick **112, 113, 115**
*Dogs of the British Islands* 10
Dominance 28, 56, 145, 149
Dorrian, Pat **20**, 21
Down 88
Ear
—cleaning 67
—cropping 15
—gluing 38
Ear-mite infestation 67, 115
Earthdog tests 95
*Echinococcus multilocularis* 118
Edbrios Dirmuid 19
Edbrios Duplicate 21
Edward VII 12
Energy level 40
Erin 16
Esperon 21
Esperon's Hillside Sandy 21
Establishment of type 14, 23
Estrus 149
Europe 10
Euthanasia 131
*Events Calendar* 137
Exercise 63-65
Exportation of breed 17
External parasites 108-115
Fairplay's Raging Cajun **8**, 21
Fairywell's Sergeant Pepper **19**, 21
Fairywells 21
Family dog 24
Fardarrigh kennels 21
Farm dog 65, 94
Fear 55, 143
Feces eating 155
Fédération Cynologique Internationale 134

Feeding 106
Fenced yard 51, 65
Field ability 25
*Field, The* 10
Finland 21
First aid 107
Flea **108, 109, 110, 111**, 112, **118**
Food 60, 106
—allergies 106
—intolerance 106
—preference 61
—rewards 86-87, 93
—stealing 154
—storage 60
—types 60
Galway Blazer 18
Gately, Michael and Mary 18
Gender differences 40
Gerald 17
Glen of Imaal Terrier 10, **13**, 14
Gluing ears 38
Goodfellow, Cheryle 21
Graham, William "Billy" 16, 17
Grooming 40, 66-71
Group show 135, 137
Growth rate 62
Guard dog 24-25
Handling 137
Harlequin Terrier 14
Head 30
Health
—adults 103
—puppy 38, 42, 99
—senior dog 129
Heartworm 119-120, **121**
Heel 91
Hepatitis 101, 102
Hereditary skin disorders 103
Home preparation for pup 43
Homeopathy 122-124
Honey, Linda 19
Honey, Marion 19
Hookworm **117**
Hormones 75
Horner, Tom 15
House-training 45, 76-84
—schedule 77, 82
Housing 77
Hunting 65
Identification 72-73
IGR 110, 112
Independence 26
Insect Growth Regulator 110, 112
Insurance 99
Intelligence 23, 26
Internal parasites 115-121
Ireland's terriers 9-10, 13
Irish dogs 9
Irish Kennel Club 19

Irish Terrier Club 15
—of America 18, 135
Irish Wolfhound 12
Jamison, George 14
Judge 138
Jumping up 151
Kate 10
Kelson's Tralee Benchmark 21
Kennel Club, The 15, 37
—address 134
Kentee Begraceful of
   Fairywells 21
Kerry Blue Terrier 10, 12, 13,
   14
Killiney Boy 16
Kilvara line 18
Krehl, George 14-15
Krehl, Mr. A. W. 15
Leash 47, 55, 85
Lee, Rawdon B 14
Leptospirosis 102
Lice 114
Life expectancy 128
Litter size 38
Living situations 28
Loyalty 24-25, 29
Lupus 105
MacDonald, Ian and Pat 21
MacDonald, Jeanene 19
Major 135
Mange 113-115
—mite 114
Marking territory 149
Maturity 40, 62, 128
Merrymac kennels 21
Merrymac Magical Michael
   21
Milk 61
Mites 68, 113, 114, 115
—infestation 68
Modern Dogs 14
Montgomery County show 18
Morgan 21
Mounting 149
Mullaghboy 19
Nail maintenance 66, 68
National Obedience
   Champion 140
National Obedience
   Invitational 140
Negative reinforcement 84,
   146
Neutering 102, 148-149
Newtownards Aristocrat 19
Nipping 58
Novice level 140
O'Brien, Ed 19
O'Brien, Philip 19
O'Callaghan, Jeremiah ("Jerry")
   18
Obedience class 74, 76, 93
Obedience trainer 146
Obedience Trial Champion
   140
Obedience trials 94, 138

Obesity 63, 65, 130
Off 151
Old-dog syndrome 127
Old English Black-and-Tan 11-
   12
Open level 140
Origin of breed 10-11, 13
Osteoarthritis 105
Other pets 24, 28
Otodectes cynotis 115
Owner suitability 24, 28
Ownership 43
Pagan II 17
Parainfluenza 101
Parasite
—bites 105
—external 108-115
—internal 115-121
Parent club 135
Parvovirus 101, 102
Peggy 17
Personality 9, 23, 30, 40
Physical characteristics 30
Playboy 17
Plucking 66
Pollen allergies 105
Poppy 17
Positive reinforcement 76, 84,
   144-146
Possessiveness 47
Praise 76, 86-87, 93, 145
Pretty Lass 17
Preventative medicine 99
Psoroptes bovis 114
Punishment 59, 81, 84, 146
Puppy
—appearance 38, 40, 42
—diet 61
—exercise 65
—family introduction to 52
—first night home 53
—grooming 66
—growth 62
—health 38, 42, 99
—ownership 41
—personality 42
—problems 54, 56, 58
—selection 36
—training 54, 75
Puppy-proofing 50, 53
Rabies 102
Red coat color 11
Red Devil 11, 13, 18
Registration of breed 13
Reserve Winners Bitch 136
Reserve Winners Dog 136
Rewards 84, 86-87, 93
Rhabditis 116
Rhipicephalus sanguineus 115
Richardson, H D 14
Rockledge kennels 19
Rockledge's Mick of Meath 19
Rough and Ready's Wild
   Irishman 19
Roundworm 115

Safety 50, 78, 81
—harness 71
—in the yard 51, 65
Sayres, Ed (Pop), Sr. 19
Scotch terrier 12-13, 16
Scottish Terrier 10
Seasonal cycles 149
Senior 128
—diet 63, 103, 130
—health care 129
—symptoms 131
Separation anxiety 58, 130,
   146
Separation of breeds 11, 14
Sexual behavior 148
Show
—classes at 136
—potential 40, 134
—types of 135
Sit 87
Size 30
Skin problems 103-105
Skye Terrier 10
Slasher 14
Smile 24, 28
Socialization 54, 144
Soft Coated Wheaten Terrier
   10, 12, 13, 14
Spaying 102, 148
Specialty show 135
Sport 14
Sporter 15
Standard 30, 134
—American Kennel Club 30
Stately Lady 19
Stay 89
Stealing food 154
Stinger 10
Stonehenge 10, 13, 15-16
Stripping 40, 66
Strongyloides 119
Stuaffenberg, Countess 19
Sumners, Amy and Minor 21
Sweden 21
Sweeney, Gerry 19
Sweeney, Paul 19
Tail docking 40
Tapeworm 118
Teeth 99, 103
Teltown General McKee 19
Teltown line 19
Temperament 9, 23, 25, 30,
   40, 65, 101
—puppy 42
Terriers of Ireland 9-10, 13
Thorndike's Theory of
   Learning 84
Thorndike, Dr. Edward 84
Threadworm 119
Tick 112-113, 115
Toxocara canis 116
Toys 46, 48-49, 59, 72, 80, 150
—possessiveness with 47
Tracheobronchitis 102
Tracking 95, 140

Tracking Dog 140
Tracking Dog Champion 140
Dog Excellent 140
Trainability 24, 26
Training 24, 26, 56
—commands 87-93
—consistency 89
—crate 76-84
—equipment 85
—obedience 94
—puppy 54
Traveling 71-72
Treats 86-87, 93
Trichuris vulpis 118
Trimming 40, 67
Tschokkinen, Jetta 21
Type 14, 23
United States 18
United States Dog Agility
   Assoc. Inc. 141
Utility Dog 139
Utility Dog Excellent 140
Utility level 140
Vacations 72
Vaccinations 52, 55, 101
Variable ratio reward system
   93
Versatile Surface Tracking
   140
Vet 51, 97, , 103, 115, 128, 142
—insurance 99
—specialist 97, 105
Visiting the litter 38
Walker, Mrs. Helen
   Whitehouse 138
Waller, Lucy 18
Walsh, J. H. 10, 13, 15-16
Wandering 149
War workers 17, 28
Ward, George 19
Watchdog 23
Water 64, 80
Waterhouse, Mr. 16
Watson, James 14
Watterson, Mr. T. 21
Weaning 62, 99
West Highland White Terrier 10
Westminster Kennel Club
   show 18
Whining 53, 58
Whipworm 118-119
Wild Irishman 13
Windeire Northern Jet Stream
   21
Winners Bitch 136
Winners Dog 136
With children 24-25, 29, 56
With other dogs 94-95, 141,
   144
With other pets 28, 41, 55
With strangers 24
Working ability 23
World War I 17, 25
Yard 51, 65
Youatt 13

# My Irish Terrier

PUT YOUR PUPPY'S FIRST PICTURE HERE

Dog's Name _____

Date _____ Photographer _____